PILON

KINGS &
QUEENS
of
ENGLAND & SCOTLAND

D0956197

KINGS & QUEENS
of
ENGLAND & SCOTLAND

PLANTAGENET SOMERSET FRY

LONDON, NEW YORK, MELBOURNE,
MUNICH, AND DELHI

Produced for Dorling Kindersley Limited by
Design Revolution, Queens Park Villa,
30 West Drive, Brighton, East Sussex BN2 2GE
EDITORIAL MANAGER Ian Whitelaw
DESIGNERS Andy Ashdown, Neal Johnson
EDITOR Julie Whitaker

SENIOR MANAGING EDITOR Krystyna Mayer
DEPUTY ART DIRECTOR Carole Ash
DTP DESIGNER Bridget Roseberry
PRODUCTION MANAGER Maryann Webster

First American Edition, 1999
Reprinted 2002, Second Edition 2006, reprinted with revisions 2011

Published in the United States by
DK Publishing
375 Hudson Street
New York, New York 10014

11 12 13 14 15   10 9 8 7 6 5 4
004 – KD078 – Apr/2011

Published in Great Britain by Dorling Kindersley Limited.

A catalog record for this book is available from the Library of Congress.

ISBN 978-0-7566-8893-6

DK books are available at special discounts when purchased in bulk for sales
promotions, premiums, fund-raising, or educational use. For details, contact:
DK Publishing Special Markets, 375 Hudson Street, New York, New York 10014
or SpecialSales@dk.com

Color reproduction by GRB Editrice, Verona, Italy
Printed and bound by L. Rex Printing Co. Ltd, China

Discover more at
www.dk.com

Contents

CHAPTER ONE

THE
FIRST ENGLISH KINGS

c. 600–1066

THE ROMANS ENDED direct rule of England in the fifth century, and by the early seventh century the country had split into seven warring kingdoms. One of these finally triumphed in 829, producing Ecgberht, the first King of England.

VIKING INVASIONS

By the ninth century England was suffering under the onslaught of Viking raids. These raids continued for more than two centuries, and considerably disrupted the country. The Vikings were not entirely victorious, however, for they faced powerful opposition from the Anglo-Saxon kings. The greatest of these, and the only one in all English history to be called "the Great", was Alfred, who, with his successors, kept the Vikings at bay, consolidated the supremacy of the Wessex kings over the whole of England, and improved the administration of the country.

FIT FOR A KING *Edward the Confessor and his nobles are waited upon at a royal banquet. Despite his Saxon origins, Edward preferred the company of his Norman advisers.*

EARLY SAXON KINGS

600–871

THE ANGLO-SAXON occupiers of England had completed the process of driving the Celts out of the country by 613. Thereafter the territory was divided into seven kingdoms: Kent, Sussex, Essex, East Anglia, Wessex, Mercia, and Northumbria, collectively known as The Heptarchy. Some of the kingdoms, most notably Kent and Northumbria, fought to convert their neighbours to Christianity, brought to England by St. Augustine in 597.

THE FIRST KING OF ENGLAND

The seven kingdoms were all intent on establishing supremacy over, or defending themselves from, their neighbours. Northumbria was the first to gain the upper hand, followed by Mercia and then Wessex. Ecgberht became King of Wessex in 802. He steadily increased the power and influence of Wessex, and in 825 defeated the Mercians at the Battle of Ellandun. Four years later, Northumbria submitted to him, and from 829 Ecgberht was recognized by his fellow kings as King of all England. His grandson, Alfred the Great, consolidated these gains.

THE ARTS AND ARCHITECTURE

Between 600 and 1066, Anglo-Saxon England produced a number of fine scholars, many of whom enjoyed an impressive reputation throughout Europe. The most notable of these was Baeda, or the Venerable Bede (673–735), an English monk and historian who lived in the kingdom

EVENTS OF THE PERIOD 770–757

◆ **597** St. Augustine settles in Canterbury and begins the conversion of the Kingdom of Kent to Christianity.

◆ **613** Led by Aethelfrith of Northumbria, the English defeat the Celts at the Battle of Chester.

◆ **617** Raedwald of East Anglia dies and is laid to rest in his burial ship at Sutton Hoo in Suffolk.

◆ **617** Northumbria establishes its supremacy over the other six kingdoms of England.

◆ **627** Paulinus, a Roman missionary and assistant to St. Augustine, converts Edwin of Northumbria to Christianity, and is made Archbishop of York.

◆ **641** Oswy becomes King of Northumbria and during the following 30 years unites the Northumbrian provinces.

◆ **685** Ecgfrith of Northumbria is defeated

and killed by the Picts at the Battle of Nechtansmere in Scotland; Northumbrian power begins to wane.

◆ **716** Aethelbald becomes King of Mercia and over the next 40 years Mercia becomes the dominant kingdom in the land.

◆ **731** The monk Bede completes the writing of his *Ecclesiastical History of the English Nation*.

◆ **757** Offa becomes the King of Mercia.

SILVER PENNY
This coin from the ninth century bears the head of King Ecgberht of Wessex.

of Northumbria. His most important work was the *Ecclesiastical History of the English Nation*, which began with a short description of Celtic Britain and outlined the events of the Roman occupation of Britain. Although it was once thought that the Saxons did not build in stone, it is now known that the advance of Christianity throughout England during and after the seventh century was marked by the construction of many churches and some small cathedrals made of stone.

EVENTS OF THE PERIOD 758–871

◆ **779** Offa defeats the West Saxons at Benson and is regarded by many as overlord of England.

◆ **780** Offa begins the construction of a great defensive dyke on the border between England and Wales to thwart border raids by the Celtic Welsh.

◆ **787** The Vikings make their first raids on the English coasts.

◆ **794** Charlemagne and Offa sign an agreement to encourage trade between England and Europe.

◆ **802** Ecgberht becomes King of Wessex, which begins to supplant Mercia as the dominant kingdom in England.

◆ **825** Ecgberht of Wessex defeats the Mercians at the Battle of Ellandun.

◆ **829** Northumbria submits to Ecgberht, and Ecgberht becomes, in effect, King of all England.

◆ **836** Ecgberht defeats a Danish invasion force at Hingston Down.

◆ **839** Aethelwulf becomes King of Wessex on the death of Ecgberht.

◆ **866** Aethelred I becomes King of Wessex and the Danes conquer East Anglia.

◆ **871** Aethelred I dies fighting the Danes at Merton and is succeeded by Alfred the Great (grandson of Ecgberht) as King of Wessex.

ALFRED THE GREAT

871–899

ALFRED ACCEDED TO THE THRONE of Wessex upon the death of his brother Aethelred in 871. Over the next few years he spent much time fighting off Viking invasions until, in 886, he captured London and was finally accepted by Saxon and Dane alike as King of all England. Alfred reformed and codified Saxon law, promoted a revival in learning, and instigated the compilation of the famous *Anglo-Saxon Chronicle*.

THE GREAT KING

The only English king to be known as Great, Alfred was the youngest son of King Aethelwulf. By the time he acceded to the throne in 871, Alfred had already shown himself to be a self-confident leader. Healthy, well-educated, decisive, and full of initiative, he was not afraid to consult colleagues and seek consensus whenever possible.

RELIGIOUS INSPIRATION

As a boy, Alfred was taken twice to visit the Pope in Rome. He learned to read and write in his teens and developed a profound interest in learning and a reverence of religion. Thus, when he turned to domestic reconstruction after defeating the Vikings, Alfred devoted much of his energy to reviving the schools and monasteries, and translating important Latin works into Anglo-Saxon himself, notably Bede's *Ecclesiastical History of the English Nation* and St. Augustine's *Soliloquies*.

EVENTS OF THE REIGN

- ◆ **871** Alfred succeeds his elder brother Aethelred as King of Wessex.
- ◆ **878** The Danes invade Wessex. Alfred takes refuge on the Isle of Athelney and prepares his forces against the Great Army of Guthrum. The apocryphal story about Alfred burning the cakes occurs during this period.
- ◆ **876** Southern Northumbria is colonized by the Danes.

- ◆ **877** Mercia is partitioned between the English and the Danes.
- ◆ **878** Danes under Guthrum attack Wessex. Alfred is driven out.
- ◆ **878** Alfred defeats Guthrum's army at Ethandune in Wessex.
- ◆ **878** Treaty of Wedmore divides England into two, and makes Alfred overlord of both halves.
- ◆ **886** Alfred captures and rebuilds London; he is now

recognized by Saxons and Danes alike as the King of all England.
- ◆ **890s** Alfred builds the first permanent fleet of warships in England, ready to engage Viking ships.
- ◆ **891** Alfred starts to compile the *Anglo-Saxon Chronicle*. Possibly derived from earlier chronicles, the *Chronicle* is written in Anglo-Saxon, the language spoken by the people, rather than Latin, the

👑 BIOGRAPHY

◆ **Born** Wantage, Oxon, 846/9, fourth son of Aethelwulf, King of Wessex, and Osburga of Hampshire.
◆ **Married** Aethelswitha of Gainas and Mercia, Winchester, 868/9, 6 children.
◆ **Acceded** 23 April 871.
◆ **Crowned** (if at all) Kingston-upon-Thames, Surrey.
◆ **Died** Probably in Wessex, 25/26/28 Oct 899, aged 50/53.

REVERED KING

This statue of Alfred the Great, acknowledged as a strong and righteous ruler, stands in his birthplace of Wantage, in Oxfordshire.

language of the Church. It outlines political, social, and economic events.
◆ **894–5** Alfred translates Orosius's *Historia Adversus Paganos* and Bede's *Ecclesiastical History of the English Nation* into Anglo-Saxon.
◆ **899** Death of Alfred, probably in Wessex.

SAXONS & VIKINGS

899–1016

ENGLAND WAS OFTEN at war with Viking invaders from Scandinavia during the tenth century. Although most Danes had been expelled by 975, raids on England began again just five years later. The Danish king, Sweyn Forkbeard, seized the kingdom from Aethelred II in 1013.

INVADERS FROM THE SEA

The Vikings were seafaring adventurers from Scandinavia who crossed the North Sea in sail- and oar-powered longboats to invade Britain and Ireland. Their attacks began at the end of the eighth century and continued on and off until the 1060s. They built settlements in many parts of the country, especially in coastal areas.

Although the Vikings brought terror and violence to many parts of Britain, they were more than savage and illiterate warriors. They had a strong sense of justice, developed municipal government, produced fine works of art, and many were eventually converted to Christianity by the Saxons.

ATHELSTAN
Crowned in 925, Athelstan came to be recognized as King of all England.

EVENTS OF THE PERIOD 899–1016

◆ **899** Edward the Elder accedes to the throne of Wessex after the death of Alfred the Great.

◆ **918** Edward the Elder subdues the Danes of East Anglia.

◆ **925** Athelstan becomes King of all England.

◆ **937** Athelstan defeats a confederation of Danes, Irish, and Scots at the Battle of Brunanburh.

◆ **939** Edmund I becomes King of England.

◆ **946** Eadred I becomes King of England.

◆ **954** Eric Bloodaxe, Danish King of Northumbria, is killed.

◆ **959** Eadgar the Peaceable accedes to throne.

◆ **975** Edward the Martyr becomes King of England.

◆ **978** Edward is killed by agents of Aethelred, who succeeds as Aethelred II.

◆ **994** Sweyn Forkbeard, King of Denmark, besieges London, but withdraws.

◆ **1002** The Massacre of St. Brice's Day.

◆ **1003** Sweyn Forkbeard invades England again.

◆ **1013** Aethelred flees to Normandy and Sweyn becomes King of England.

◆ **1014** Sweyn Forkbeard dies and is succeeded by his son, Canute. Aethelred is restored to the throne.

◆ **1016** Aethelred dies, and his son, Edmund Ironside, fights for his inheritance against Canute.

THE AGE OF CANUTE

1016–1066

WHEN AETHELRED DIED IN 1016 there were two claimants to the throne – his son, Edmund Ironside, and Sweyn's son, Canute. After several battles, the two agreed to divide the country between them. However, Edmund soon died and Canute became King. After Canute's death in 1035, the throne passed to his two sons – Harold and Harthacanute – and then, in 1042, to Edward the Confessor, who reigned until 1066.

A VIKING KING

Ruler of England, Denmark, and Norway from 1016 to 1035, Canute brought much-needed stability to the affairs of England during his reign. Although a Viking, he treated Dane and Saxon alike and wisely appointed Englishmen to positions of importance in the Church and at court. His modernization of the country's laws bear this out and he may be fairly described as one of the best kings England has ever had. After his death in 1035, Canute was mourned by both Saxon and Dane.

HEADS OF STATE
These 11th-century coins show (top left to bottom right) Kings Aethelred II, Canute, Harold Harefoot, and Harthacanute.

EVENTS OF THE PERIOD 1016–1066

- ◆ **1016** Aethelred II dies and the Saxons choose his son, Edmund Ironside, to succeed him. The Danes choose Canute.
- ◆ **1016** At the Battle of Ashingdon, in Essex, Canute defeats Edmund and they agree to divide the kingdom into two.
- ◆ **1016** Edmund dies and Canute becomes King.
- ◆ **1035** Canute dies and Harold Harefoot usurps the throne from his half-

brother, Harthacanute, the rightful heir.
- ◆ **1040** Harold Harefoot dies and Harthacanute accedes to the throne.
- ◆ **1042** Harthacanute dies and is succeeded by Edward the Confessor, son of Aethelred II.
- ◆ **1051** Edward banishes the rebellious Godwine family from England.
- ◆ **1051** Edward promises the throne to William, Duke of Normandy.

- ◆ **1052** Godwine, Earl of Wessex, returns to England.
- ◆ **1053** Godwine's son, Harold, becomes principal adviser to the King.
- ◆ **1064** Harold visits William of Normandy and swears on oath to support his claim to the throne.
- ◆ **1066** Edward dies and Harold Godwineson is chosen as successor, but William of Normandy declares the throne was promised to him.

CHAPTER TWO

THE NORMANS

1066–1154

T HE NORMANS WERE originally Vikings who settled in northwest France in the early 10th century. Taking control, they became Counts, and later Dukes, of Normandy, and they created a powerful state around the mouth of the River Seine.

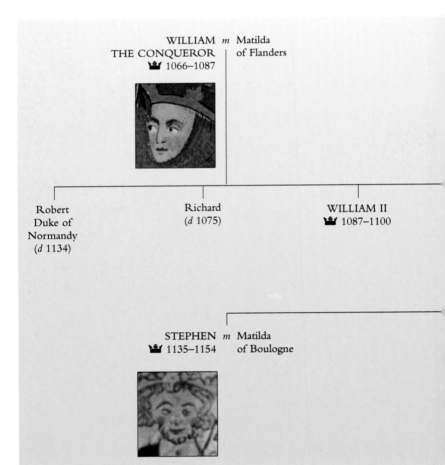

WILLIAM *m* Matilda
THE CONQUEROR | of Flanders
♛ 1066–1087

Robert
Duke of
Normandy
(*d* 1134)

Richard
(*d* 1075)

WILLIAM II
♛ 1087–1100

STEPHEN *m* Matilda
♛ 1135–1154   of Boulogne

THE NORMAN INVASION

In the middle of the 11th century, the Normans conquered both
Southern Italy and England. William, who had a claim on the
English throne, defeated the English King Harold at the Battle of
Hastings, and was crowned King on Christmas Day in 1066. A new,
alien aristocracy was imposed upon more than two million English
people, and England was given firm, but arrogant, government.
The Normans dispossessed many of the Anglo-Saxon landowners,
pressed the peasantry into service on their new feudal territories,
and treated their Anglo-Saxon subjects with contempt, but they
also taught better farming, developed the economy, put an end to
Viking raids, and built many fine stone cathedrals and churches.

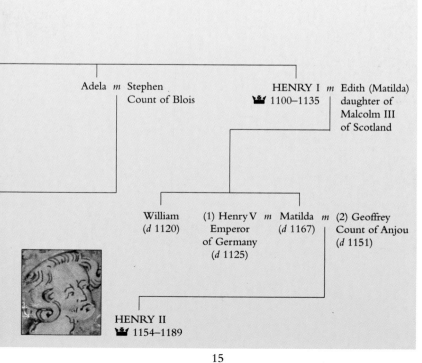

Adela *m* Stephen
Count of Blois

HENRY I *m* Edith (Matilda)
♔ 1100–1135   daughter of
Malcolm III
of Scotland

William
(*d* 1120)

(1) Henry V *m* Matilda *m* (2) Geoffrey
Emperor   (*d* 1167)   Count of Anjou
of Germany   (*d* 1151)
(*d* 1125)

HENRY II
♔ 1154–1189

WILLIAM I

1066–1087

PROMISED THE ENGLISH THRONE by Edward the Confessor, but denied it by Harold II, William brought a Norman army over to England in 1066. After defeating Harold at the Battle of Hastings, William subdued the local population by confiscating Anglo-Saxon estates and giving them to his Norman followers.

♛ BIOGRAPHY

◆ **Born** Falaise Castle, Normandy, France, 1027/28, illegitimate son of Robert of Normandy and Arlette of Conteville.
◆ **Married** Matilda of Flanders, Cathedral of Notre Dame d'Eu, Normandy, 1050/52, 10 children.
◆ **Acceded** 14 Oct 1066.
◆ **Crowned** Westminster Abbey, 25 Dec 1066.
◆ **Died** Rouen, Normandy, 9 Sept 1087, aged 59/60.

LATE LIKENESS
This portrait of William is unlikely to be realistic as it was not drawn until the 13th century, appearing in a manuscript depicting William at the Battle of Hastings.

EVENTS OF THE REIGN

◆ **1066** William and his Norman army defeat Harold II and the Saxons at the Battle of Hastings. Harold is killed and, after subduing the rest of the country, William is crowned King of England.
◆ **1067** William suppresses a Saxon revolt in the southwest of England.
◆ **1068–9** William puts down revolt led by Edwin and Morcar and lays waste to the northern counties.

◆ **1071** William defeats a revolt led by Hereward the Wake in East Anglia, thus putting an end to Saxon resistance to his rule.
◆ **1072** William invades Scotland and compels Malcolm III to pay homage to him.
◆ **1079** William begins the construction of a Norman Cathedral at Winchester.
◆ **1079** Robert, William's eldest son, leads a rebellion in Normandy, but is

defeated by his father at the Battle of Gerberoi and his life is spared.
◆ **1080** William refuses to pay homage to the Pope.
◆ **1085** William orders a survey of the shires of England; the information is recorded in the Domesday Book, which is completed the following year.
◆ **1087** William dies of his injuries after falling from his horse while besieging the French city of Nantes.

WILLIAM II

1087–1100

THE THIRD SON OF William the Conqueror, William II was named heir by his father in place of his elder brother, Robert, who received the Duchy of Normandy. He successfully crushed a rebellion in Normandy early in his rule, as well as repulsing two invasions led by Malcolm III of Scotland.

♚ BIOGRAPHY

◆ **Born** Normandy, 1056/60, third son of William I and Matilda of Flanders.
◆ **Acceded** 9 Sept 1087.
◆ **Crowned** Westminster Abbey, 26 Sept 1087.
◆ **Died** New Forest, Hampshire, 2 Aug 1100, aged 40/44.

HUNTER'S DEATH

William II was also known as Rufus because of his fiery red complexion. An illustration created at the time depicts him at the moment of his death. He was killed by an arrow while out hunting with friends in the New Forest in August 1100.

EVENTS OF THE REIGN

◆ **1087** William II accedes to the throne on the death of his father, William I.
◆ **1088** William crushes a baronial rebellion in Normandy led by his uncle, Odo of Bayeux, who supports the claims of William's brother, Robert of Normandy, to the English throne.
◆ **1089** Ranulf Flambard, leading adviser to William, is appointed Justiciar (the King's main judicial officer). He begins to levy heavy taxes on the church.
◆ **1090** William leads an invasion of Normandy in an attempt to subdue his brother, Robert.
◆ **1091** William defeats an invasion of England led by Malcolm III of Scotland.
◆ **1092** Carlisle is captured from Scotland and Cumberland is annexed.
◆ **1093** Malcolm III and the Scots invade England again, but they are defeated and Malcolm is killed at the Battle of Alnwick.
◆ **1095** William suppresses revolt in Northumbria.
◆ **1098** William suppresses a Welsh rebellion against the Norman border lords.
◆ **1100** William is killed by an arrow while out hunting in the New Forest. Supposedly an accident, it has been suggested that he was shot deliberately on the instructions of his brother Henry.

HENRY I

1100–1135

ALTHOUGH HENRY SEIZED the Crown under suspicious circumstances, he ruled well. Promising good governance, he introduced a number of important reforms, developing the King's Council to settle disputes between the Crown and its tenants, and expanding the system of travelling justices in the shires.

♛ BIOGRAPHY

◆ **Born** Selby, Yorkshire, Sept 1068, fourth son of William I and Matilda.
◆ **Acceded** 2 Aug 1100.
◆ **Crowned** Westminster Abbey, 5 Aug 1100.
◆ **Married** Edith of Scotland, 11 Nov 1100, 4 children; Adela of Louvain, 29 Jan 1121.
◆ **Died** Rouen, Normandy, 1/2 Dec 1135, aged 67.

BEREAVED FATHER
This drawing of Henry I shows a sombre and sad man, as it illustrates a manuscript describing the loss at sea of his only legitimate son, William.

EVENTS OF THE REIGN

◆ **1100** Henry I succeeds his brother, William II.
◆ **1100** Henry issues a Charter of Liberties, pledging good governance.
◆ **1100** Henry marries Edith, daughter of Malcolm III of Scotland. She adopts the extra name of Matilda, which is more acceptable to the English barons.
◆ **1101** Robert of Normandy invades England in an attempt to wrest the English throne from his brother, Henry. After failing, he signs the Treaty of Alton, which confirms Henry as King of England and Robert as Duke of Normandy.
◆ **1106** War breaks out between Henry and Robert. Henry defeats Robert at the Battle of Tinchebrai, imprisons him in Cardiff Castle, and takes control of Normandy.
◆ **1118** Death of Matilda.
◆ **1120** Henry's son and heir, William, is drowned at sea. Henry's daughter, Matilda, becomes heir.
◆ **1121** Henry marries Adela of Louvain.
◆ **1126** Henry persuades the barons to accept Matilda as his lawful successor to the throne.
◆ **1128** Matilda marries Geoffrey Plantagenet, Count of Anjou.
◆ **1135** Henry I dies of food poisoning.

STEPHEN

1135–1154

O N HENRY I'S DEATH in 1135, Stephen usurped the throne from Matilda, Henry's daughter, and most of his reign was marked by civil war with the rival claimant. Order was not restored until 1153, when her son, Henry of Anjou, compelled the barons to recognize him as the heir to the throne.

👑 BIOGRAPHY

- **Born** Blois, France, 1096/7, son of Stephen, Count of Blois and Adela of Flanders.
- **Married** Matilda of Boulogne, 1125, 5 children.
- **Acceded** 22 Dec 1135.
- **Crowned** Westminster Abbey, 26 Dec 1135.
- **Died** 25 Oct 1154, Dover, Kent, aged 57/58.

THE HUNTER

In a manuscript illustration of the time, Stephen is shown wearing a gauntlet and feeding a falcon, hunting being one of his favourite pastimes.

EVENTS OF THE REIGN

- **1135** Stephen usurps the throne from Matilda, Henry I's daughter.
- **1136** The Earl of Norfolk leads the first rebellion against Stephen.
- **1138** Robert, Earl of Gloucester, an illegitimate son of Henry I, deserts Stephen and pledges allegiance to Matilda.
- **1138** David I of Scotland invades England in support of his niece, Matilda, but is defeated.

- **1139** Matilda leaves France for England.
- **1141** Matilda's forces take Stephen prisoner, and Matilda is made queen.
- **1141** Earl Robert is captured and exchanged for Stephen's freedom.
- **1145** Stephen defeats Matilda's forces at the Battle of Faringdon.
- **1148** Matilda abandons cause and leaves England.
- **1151** Matilda's son, Henry Plantagenet,

succeeds his father as Count of Anjou.
- **1153** Henry of Anjou lands in England, and gathers support for further war against Stephen.
- **1153** Henry and Stephen agree terms for ending the civil war. Under the terms of the Treaty of Westminster, Stephen is to remain King for life, but thereafter the throne passes to Henry.
- **1154** Stephen dies.

CHAPTER THREE

THE PLANTAGENETS

1154–1399

T HE SURNAME OF THIS remarkable family derives from the nickname borne by Geoffrey, Count of Anjou, between 1129 and 1251. Geoffrey, the father of Henry II, wore a sprig of flowering broom (*Planta genista*) as his personal badge.

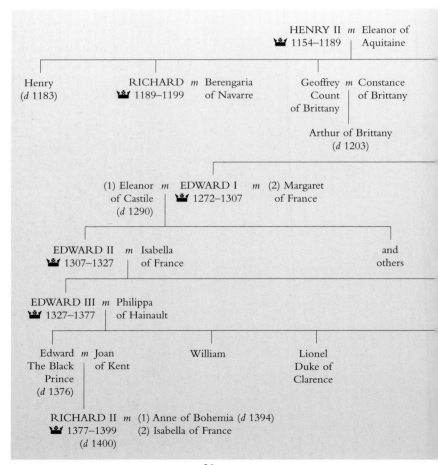

HENRY II *m* Eleanor of
👑 1154–1189 | Aquitaine

Henry | RICHARD *m* Berengaria | Geoffrey *m* Constance
(*d* 1183) | 👑 1189–1199 of Navarre | Count of Brittany | of Brittany

Arthur of Brittany
(*d* 1203)

(1) Eleanor *m* EDWARD I *m* (2) Margaret
of Castile | 👑 1272–1307 | of France
(*d* 1290)

EDWARD II *m* Isabella | and
👑 1307–1327 | of France | others

EDWARD III *m* Philippa
👑 1327–1377 | of Hainault

Edward *m* Joan | William | Lionel
The Black | of Kent | | Duke of
Prince | | | Clarence
(*d* 1376)

RICHARD II *m* (1) Anne of Bohemia (*d* 1394)
👑 1377–1399 | (2) Isabella of France
(*d* 1400)

THE PLANTAGENET ERA

The first Plantagenet king of England was Henry II, and he is generally regarded as the greatest of them. Thirteen more kings followed him in a dynasty that ruled for 331 years, although for the last 86 years, rival families within the dynasty struggling to seize the crown took the names of Lancaster and York, even though all were Plantagenets. For much of this long period, the kings were involved in costly and largely unproductive wars with France and Scotland, and in power struggles with the over-mighty barons at home. As a dynasty, the Plantagenets made their greatest contribution in the development of English law, especially the unique Common Law, and by sponsoring a splendid architectural heritage.

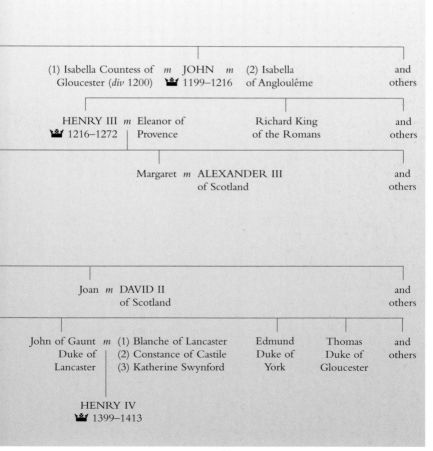

(1) Isabella Countess of   *m*   JOHN   *m*   (2) Isabella   and
Gloucester (*div* 1200)   👑 1199–1216   of Anglouléme   others

HENRY III *m* Eleanor of   Richard King   and
👑 1216–1272 │ Provence   of the Romans   others

Margaret *m* ALEXANDER III   and
of Scotland   others

Joan *m* DAVID II   and
of Scotland   others

John of Gaunt *m* (1) Blanche of Lancaster   Edmund   Thomas   and
Duke of │ (2) Constance of Castile   Duke of   Duke of   others
Lancaster │ (3) Katherine Swynford   York   Gloucester

HENRY IV
👑 1399–1413

HENRY II

1154–1189

ENRY'S SUCCESSION IN 1154 made him lord of a vast empire, and he was equipped with all the intellectual and physical qualities to rule it well. Henry began by destroying the castles built by rebellious barons during Stephen's reign, and then set about regulating the power of the Church. Although the latter years of his reign were plagued by family revolts, his vast empire was still intact when he died in 1189.

THE ANGEVIN EMPIRE

When Henry II became King of England in 1154 he was already Count of Anjou and of Touraine, and Duke of Normandy and of Aquitaine. As such, he was lord of an empire that stretched from the Cheviot Hills down to the Pyrenees, his territories in France exceeding even those of the French king. Known as the Angevin Empire (because the country of Anjou lay at its heart), this vast domain was held together by diplomacy and force of arms, and remained intact up to the death of Richard I in 1199.

HENRY II AND THE CHURCH

In 1164 Henry set out various Church reforms in the Constitutions of Clarendon. These included the proposal that the clergy or others associated with the Church, if charged with a criminal offence, should be tried in the civil courts, and that no appeal could be made to Rome without the King's consent. Despite fierce opposition from the Church, these reforms

EVENTS OF THE REIGN 1154–1166

◆ **1154** Henry II accedes to the throne at the age of 21 upon the death of his second cousin, Stephen.

◆ **1155** Henry appoints Thomas à Becket as Chancellor of England, a post that he holds for seven years.

◆ **1155** Pope Adrian IV issues the papal bull *Laudabiliter*, which gives Henry dispensation to invade Ireland and bring the Irish Church under

the control of the Church of Rome.

◆ **1162** On the death of Archbishop Theobald, Henry appoints Thomas à Becket to the archbishopric of Canterbury in the hope that he will help introduce Church reforms.

◆ **1164** Henry introduces the Constitutions of Clarendon, which place limitations on the Church's jurisdiction over crimes

committed by the clergy. The Pope refuses to approve the Constitutions, so Thomas à Becket refuses to sign them. This leads to a violent quarrel between Henry and Becket, after which the latter goes into exile in France.

◆ **1166** The Assize of Clarendon establishes trial by jury for the first time.

◆ **1166** Dermot McMurrough, King of Leinster in Ireland, appeals

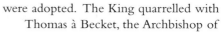

were adopted. The King quarrelled with Thomas à Becket, the Archbishop of Canterbury, over the new laws and, although the two men were reconciled, they again quarrelled in 1170. In exasperation, Henry cried out: "Will not someone rid me of this turbulent priest?" Four of Henry's knights responded to the King's outburst and set off for Canterbury, where they pursued the archbishop into his cathedral and murdered him in front of the altar.

♛ BIOGRAPHY

◆ **Born** Le Mans, Anjou, 5 Mar 1133, the first son of Geoffrey Plantagenet and Matilda.
◆ **Married** Eleanor of Aquitaine, Bordeaux Cathedral, 18 May 1152, 8 children.
◆ **Acceded** 19 Dec 1154.
◆ **Crowned** Westminster Abbey, 19 Dec 1154.
◆ **Died** Chinon Castle, France, 6 July 1189, aged 56.

LORD OF AN EMPIRE
Tough and athletic, Henry II was strongly built, with a leonine head, freckled face, and red hair.

EVENTS OF THE REIGN 1166–1189

to Henry to help him oppose a confederation of other Irish kings. In response to the appeal, Henry sends a force led by Richard de Clare, Earl of Pembroke, thereby beginning the English settlement of Ireland.
◆ **1168** English scholars expelled from Paris settle in Oxford, where they found a university.
◆ **1170** Pope Alexander III threatens England with an

interdict and forces Henry to a formal reconciliation with Becket. However, the two of them quarrel again when Becket publishes papal letters voiding Henry's Constitutions of Clarendon. Becket is killed at the high altar in Canterbury Cathedral on 29 December by four of Henry's knights.
◆ **1171** Henry invades Ireland and receives homage from the King of

Leinster and the other Irish kings. Henry is accepted as Lord of Ireland.
◆ **1171** At the Council of Cashel, Henry makes the Irish clergy submit to the authority of Rome.
◆ **1173** Canonization of Thomas à Becket.
◆ **1173–4** Henry's sons – Henry, Richard, and Geoffrey – lead an unsuccessful rebellion against their father.
◆ **1189** Death of Henry.

RICHARD I

1189–1199

RICHARD I CAPTURED THE POPULAR imagination with his crusading zeal and his chivalry. However, England saw him for only seven months of a ten-year reign, and paid dearly for his faraway campaigns and the huge ransom that secured his freedom, only to see him return to France, where he died.

♛ BIOGRAPHY

◆ **Born** Beaumont Palace, Oxford, 8 Sept 1157, third son of Henry II and Eleanor of Aquitaine.
◆ **Acceded** 2 Sept 1189.
◆ **Crowned** Westminster Abbey, 2 Sept 1189.
◆ **Married** Berengaria of Navarre, Chapel of St. George, Limassol, Cyprus, 12 May 1191.
◆ **Died** Chalus, France, 6 April 1199, aged 41.

LIONHEART
Richard was tall, long-legged, athletic, and powerful. A well-educated man, he showed tremendous personal courage in battle and was justifiably known as the Lionheart (Coeur de Lion). This effigy marks his final resting place at Fontevrault Abbey in France.

EVENTS OF THE REIGN

◆ **1189** Richard I becomes King of England upon the death of Henry II.
◆ **1189** William Longchamp is appointed Chancellor of England and governs the country during Richard's absence abroad.
◆ **1189** Richard sets out with Philip of France on the Third Crusade to the Holy Land.
◆ **1191** William Longchamp falls from power and Richard's

brother, John, takes over the government.
◆ **1191** Richard captures the city of Acre, Palestine, and defeats Saladin at Arsouf, near Jaffa.
◆ **1192** Richard reaches an agreement with Saladin to guarantee Christians safe pilgrimage to Jerusalem.
◆ **1192** On his way back to England from Palestine, Richard is captured and handed over to Henry VI, Emperor of Germany.

Henry demands a ransom of 100,000 marks from England for Richard's release from prison.
◆ **1194** The ransom is raised in England.
◆ **1194** Richard is released from captivity. He returns to England for a brief period, before leaving to fight in France, never to return to his homeland.
◆ **1199** Richard is mortally wounded in battle at Chalus, in France.

JOHN
1199–1216

JOHN'S LOSS OF THE FRENCH dominions, his disputes with Rome, and a high level of taxation had the English nobility up in arms against him. In 1215 they forced the King to sign the Magna Carta, guaranteeing their rights in relation to those of the crown. This led to civil war, which only ended with John's death.

👑 BIOGRAPHY

◆ **Born** Beaumont Palace, Oxford, 24 Dec 1166, fourth son of Henry II and Eleanor.
◆ **Married** Isabella of Gloucester, Marlborough, 29 Aug 1189, no children; Isabella of Angoulême, 24 Aug 1200, 5 children.
◆ **Acceded** 27 May 1199.
◆ **Crowned** Westminster Abbey, 27 May 1199.
◆ **Died** Newark Castle, Lincolnshire, 18/19 Oct 1216, aged 49.

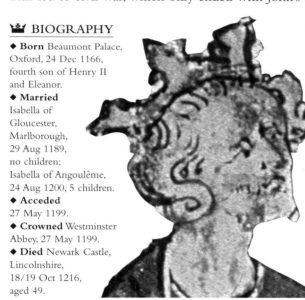

ENERGETIC KING
Despite his problems with France and the English barons, recent historical research suggests that John was a keen administrator, a good general, an astute diplomat, and a hard-working and intelligent ruler with a strong sense of justice.

EVENTS OF THE REIGN

◆ **1199** John accedes to the throne on the death of his brother, Richard I.
◆ **1204** England loses most of its possessions in France.
◆ **1206** John refuses to accept Stephen Langton as Archbishop of Canterbury.
◆ **1208** Pope Innocent III issues an Interdict against England, banning all church services except baptisms and funerals.
◆ **1209** Pope Innocent III excommunicates John for his confiscation of ecclesiastical property.
◆ **1212** Innocent III declares that John is no longer the rightful King.
◆ **1213** John submits to the Pope's demands.
◆ **1214** Philip Augustus of France defeats the English at the Battle of Bouvines.
◆ **1215** John meets the English barons at Runnymede, agrees to their demands, and seals the Magna Carta.
◆ **1215** The Pope decrees that John need not adhere to the Magna Carta, and civil war breaks out.
◆ **1216** The barons seek French aid in their fight against John; Prince Louis of France captures the Tower of London.
◆ **1216** John loses his war chest of cash and jewels in the Wash, on the east coast.
◆ **1216** John dies at Newark and is buried in Worcester Cathedral.

HENRY III

1216–1272

URING HENRY'S MINORITY, England was ruled wisely by two regents. However, in 1227 Henry took control and years of misrule followed. In 1265, Simon de Montfort summoned the first English parliament, but he was killed at the Battle of Evesham. The King reassumed control until his death.

👑 BIOGRAPHY

◆ **Born** Winchester, 1 Oct 1207, first son of John and Isabella.
◆ **Acceded** 28 Oct 1216.
◆ **Crowned** Gloucester Cathedral, 28 Oct 1216; Westminster Abbey, 17 May 1220.
◆ **Married** Eleanor of Provence, Canterbury, 14 Jan 1236, 9 children.
◆ **Died** Westminster, 16 Nov 1272, aged 65.

UNPOPULAR MONARCH

Henry III had few of the personal qualities required to command respect. Unmartial, untrustworthy, childishly fickle, and prone to petulance, he alienated enemies and advisers alike.

EVENTS OF THE REIGN

◆ **1216** Henry III is crowned King at the age of nine. England is ruled temporarily by two regents, Hubert de Burgh and William the Marshal.
◆ **1222** De Burgh successfully puts down an insurrection supporting the French king Louis VIII's claim to the throne.
◆ **1227** Henry takes full control of the government of England, but retains de Burgh as his main adviser.

◆ **1232** Hubert de Burgh is dismissed as adviser.
◆ **1236** Henry marries Eleanor of Provence.
◆ **1238** Simon de Montfort marries Henry's sister, Eleanor.
◆ **1258** The English barons, led by de Montfort, rebel against Henry's misgovernment. They present a list of grievances to Henry, who signs the Provisions of Oxford, which limit royal power.

◆ **1261** Henry repudiates the Provisions of Oxford.
◆ **1264** The Baron's War breaks out. De Montfort defeats Henry at Lewes.
◆ **1265** Simon de Montfort summons the first English Parliament.
◆ **1265** Some of the barons break their alliance with de Montfort and, led by Prince Edward, kill him at the Battle of Evesham.
◆ **1272** Henry III dies in the Palace of Westminster.

EDWARD I

1272–1307

Edward I is best remembered for his attempt to unite the kingdoms of England and Scotland under his personal rule, as well as for conquering Wales. In summoning a partly elected Parliament in 1295 – the so-called Model Parliament – Edward made an early attempt at representative democracy.

👑 BIOGRAPHY

◆ **Born** Westminster, 17/18 June 1239, first son of Henry III and Eleanor of Provence.
◆ **Married** Eleanor of Castile, Burgos, Spain, Oct 1254, 16 children; Margaret of France, Canterbury, 8/10 Sept 1299, 3 children.
◆ **Acceded** 20 Nov 1272.
◆ **Crowned** Westminster Abbey, 19 Aug 1274.
◆ **Died** Burgh-on-Sands, Cumbria, 7 July 1307, aged 68.

CROWNED CRUSADER
When he left on crusade in 1270, Edward was heir to the throne. He returned as king in 1274, Henry III having died two years earlier.

EVENTS OF THE REIGN

◆ **1272** Edward learns that he has succeeded to the throne on his way home from the Crusade.
◆ **1274** Edward is crowned in Westminster Abbey.
◆ **1282** Edward invades North Wales and defeats Prince Llywelyn.
◆ **1284** Independence of the Welsh is ended by the Statute of Rhuddlan.
◆ **1292** Edward chooses John Balliol to be the new King of Scotland.

◆ **1295** Model Parliament is summoned.
◆ **1295** Balliol refuses to join Edward on French campaign and forms the Auld Alliance with France.
◆ **1296** Edward invades Scotland and deposes Balliol. He then takes over the throne of Scotland and removes the Stone of Scone to Westminster.
◆ **1297** Scots rise against English rule and, led by William Wallace, defeat

Edward at the Battle of Stirling Bridge.
◆ **1298** Edward invades Scotland again and defeats William Wallace at the Battle of Falkirk.
◆ **1301** Edward makes his son Prince of Wales.
◆ **1305** William Wallace is executed in London.
◆ **1306** Robert Bruce is crowned King of Scotland.
◆ **1307** Edward attempts to invade Scotland again, but dies on his way north.

PRINCE OF WALES

1301

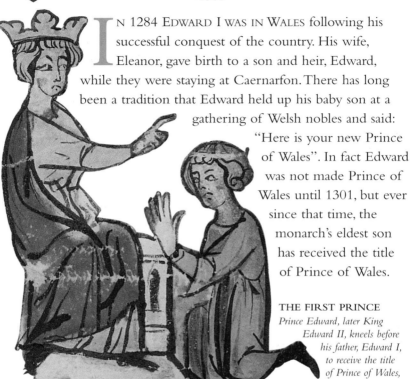

I N 1284 EDWARD I WAS IN WALES following his successful conquest of the country. His wife, Eleanor, gave birth to a son and heir, Edward, while they were staying at Caernarfon. There has long been a tradition that Edward held up his baby son at a gathering of Welsh nobles and said: "Here is your new Prince of Wales". In fact Edward was not made Prince of Wales until 1301, but ever since that time, the monarch's eldest son has received the title of Prince of Wales.

THE FIRST PRINCE
Prince Edward, later King Edward II, kneels before his father, Edward I, to receive the title of Prince of Wales, a tradition that continues to this day.

THE 21 PRINCES OF WALES

◆ **Not All Succeed**
Although it is customary for the heir to the throne to be created Prince of Wales, it does not follow that he succeeds to the throne. Seven have failed to become king, namely the Black Prince; Edward, the son of Henry VI; Edward, the son of Richard III; Arthur, the son of Henry VII; Henry Frederick, son of James I; James Stuart, the Old Pretender, whose

father, James II, fled the throne in 1688; and Frederick, son of George II.
◆ **From Prince to King**
Only 11 of the 31 kings from Edward II to the present day were first Prince of Wales, namely Richard II, Henry V, Edward V, Henry VIII, Charles I, George II, George III, George IV, Edward VII, George V, and Edward VIII. Charles II was never formally invested,

while the current Prince of Wales is still heir to the throne. The age at which each was created Prince of Wales has varied greatly: George II was only five days old, whereas George V was well into his thirties.
◆ **Princes' Motto**
Every Prince of Wales has as his motto the words adopted by the Black Prince from the King of Bohemia at the Battle of Crécy: Ich Dien, "I serve".

EDWARD II

1307–1327

ONE OF THE SADDER personalities among English monarchs, it is hard not to feel sorry for Edward II, not only for the terrible manner of his death but also for the difficulties that beset him during his 20-year reign. He was finally deposed and, in 1327, horribly murdered on his wife's orders.

♛ BIOGRAPHY

◆ **Born** Caernarfon Castle, 25 April 1284, fourth son of Edward I and Eleanor of Castile.
◆ **Acceded** 8 July 1307.
◆ **Married** Isabella of France, Boulogne, 25/28 Jan 1308, 4 children.
◆ **Crowned** Westminster Abbey, 24/25 Feb 1308.
◆ **Deposed** 20 Jan 1327.
◆ **Murdered** Berkeley Castle, 21 Sept 1327, aged 43.

TRAGIC KING
Blessed with good health, good looks, and a good brain, Edward was physically strong and enjoyed a variety of sporting interests. However, his loyalty to his friends, one of his greatest virtues, led to his downfall, for he was a poor judge of men.

EVENTS OF THE REIGN

◆ **1307** Edward II accedes to the throne on the death of his father, Edward I.
◆ **1308** Edward's favourite, Piers Gaveston, is exiled for misgovernment.
◆ **1309** Gaveston returns from exile in France.
◆ **1310** Parliament sets up a committee of Lords Ordainers to control the King and improve administration. The King's cousin, Thomas, Earl of Lancaster, takes control.

◆ **1312** Piers Gaveston is kidnapped by the King's opponents and is put to death.
◆ **1314** Edward and the English army are routed at the Battle of Bannockburn by Robert Bruce. Scottish independence is assured.
◆ **1320** Welsh border barons, father and son, both named Hugh Despenser, gain the King's favour.
◆ **1322** Barons' rebellion, led by Thomas, Earl of

Lancaster, is crushed at the Battle of Boroughbridge in Yorkshire.
◆ **1326** Edward's wife, Isabella, abandons him and with her lover, Mortimer, seizes power and deposes Edward. The Despensers are both put to death.
◆ **1327** Edward is formally deposed by Parliament in favour of Edward III, his son, and is murdered in Berkeley Castle on the orders of his wife, Isabella.

EDWARD III

1327–1377

EDWARD RULED FOR 50 YEARS, a reign dominated by the 100 Years' War with France. Edward's principal aim was to unite the nobility into a cohesive class of public servants, motivated by chivalry, enriched by the wealth he enabled them to win, and tied to the crown through marriage to his relatives.

♛ BIOGRAPHY

◆ **Born** Windsor Castle, 13 Nov 1312, first son of Edward II and Isabella of France.
◆ **Acceded** 25 Jan 1327.
◆ **Crowned** Westminster Abbey, 1 Feb 1327.
◆ **Married** Philippa of Hainault, York, 24 Jan 1328, 13 children.
◆ **Died** Surrey, 21 June 1377, aged 64.

PEOPLE'S FAVOURITE
Tall and handsome, with gold-red hair, Edward was a flamboyant, affable, and generous man. He excelled in the knightly arts, and loved hunting and falconry. He was much loved by his people.

EVENTS OF THE REIGN

◆ **1327** Edward III accedes to the throne after his father, Edward II, is formally deposed.
◆ **1330** Edward takes power after three years of government by his mother, Isabella of France, and her lover, Roger Mortimer.
◆ **1332** Parliament is divided into two houses – Lords and Commons – for the very first time.
◆ **1333** Defeat of Scottish army at Halidon Hill.

◆ **1337** Start of 100 Years' War with France.
◆ **1346** David II of Scotland invades England but is defeated at Neville's Cross and captured.
◆ **1346** French defeated at the Battle of Crécy.
◆ **1347** Edward besieges and captures Calais.
◆ **1348–50** Black Death kills one-third of the English population.
◆ **1356** Black Prince defeats French at Poitiers.

◆ **1357** David II is released from captivity and returns home to Scotland.
◆ **1376** Parliament gains right to investigate public abuses and impeach offenders; the first impeachment is of Alice Perrers, Edward's mistress, and two lords.
◆ **1376** Death of Edward, the Black Prince.
◆ **1377** Edward III dies of a stroke at Sheen Palace, Surrey, aged 64 years.

RICHARD II

1377–1399

RICHARD CAME TO THE THRONE as a ten-year-old child, and his advisers ruled the country until 1389, when Richard took control himself. At first he ruled well, presiding over a period of prosperity, but after the death of his wife, Anne, in 1394, his behaviour changed. In 1399 he was forced to abdicate.

👑 BIOGRAPHY

- **Born** Bordeaux, France, 6 Jan 1367, second son of Edward the Black Prince and Joan of Kent.
- **Acceded** 22 June 1377.
- **Crowned** Westminster Abbey, 16 July 1377.
- **Married** Anne of Bohemia, Westminster, 14/20/22 Jan 1382; Isabella of France, France, 4 Nov 1396.
- **Deposed** 19 Aug 1399.
- **Died** 6 Jan or 14 Feb 1400, aged 33.

CHILD KING
This portrait of Richard, possibly by artist André Beauneveu of Valenciennes, is the earliest known painted portrait of an English sovereign.

EVENTS OF THE REIGN

- **1377** Richard II succeeds his grandfather, Edward III; the kingdom is ruled at first by the King's uncles, John of Gaunt and Thomas of Gloucester.
- **1380** John Wycliffe begins to translate the New Testament from Greek into English.
- **1381** Poll Tax leads to the Peasants' Revolt.
- **1382** William of Wykeham founds Winchester College.

- **1387–9** Led by the Duke of Gloucester, the Lords Appellant control the government.
- **1389** Richard takes control of the government; William of Wykeham is Lord Chancellor.
- **1394** Richard leads English army to reconquer west of Ireland.
- **1397** Richard takes revenge against Lords Appellant and exiles Henry Bolingbroke.

- **1398** Chaucer finishes *The Canterbury Tales*.
- **1399** Bolingbroke becomes Duke of Lancaster on the death of John of Gaunt, but Richard seizes his possessions. Bolingbroke returns from exile to claim his inheritance and seizes the throne. Richard, who is away fighting at Leinster in Ireland, returns, but is deposed and imprisoned in Pontefract Castle, where he dies in 1400.

CHAPTER FOUR

THE HOUSE OF LANCASTER
1399–1461

A BRANCH OF THE PLANTAGENET FAMILY, the House of Lancaster was a short dynasty of three kings, all named Henry. The first, Henry IV, was the Duke of Lancaster and the eldest son of John of Gaunt, the fourth son of Edward III.

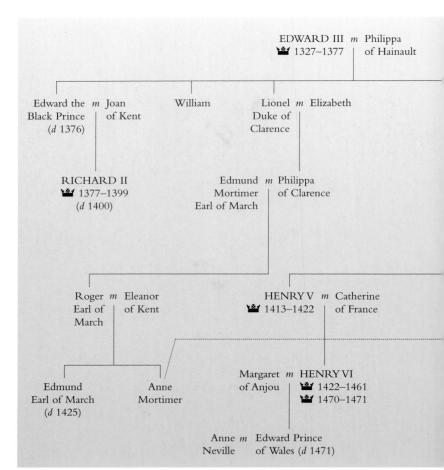

EDWARD III *m* Philippa
♛ 1327–1377 | of Hainault

Edward the *m* Joan   William   Lionel *m* Elizabeth
Black Prince | of Kent   Duke of
(*d* 1376)   Clarence

RICHARD II   Edmund *m* Philippa
♛ 1377–1399   Mortimer | of Clarence
(*d* 1400)   Earl of March

Roger *m* Eleanor   HENRY V *m* Catherine
Earl of | of Kent   ♛ 1413–1422 | of France
March

Edmund   Anne   Margaret *m* HENRY VI
Earl of March   Mortimer   of Anjou | ♛ 1422–1461
(*d* 1425)   ♛ 1470–1471

Anne *m* Edward Prince
Neville   of Wales (*d* 1471)

WARFARE AND DYNASTIC SQUABBLING

The Lancastrian period was marked by almost continual warfare. Baronial revolt and war with Welsh patriots broke out in the first decade, and dynastic war during the last, with prolonged warfare in France occupying most of the intervening four decades, when King Henry V opened the final phase of the 100 Years' War. He recovered many English possessions, but they were all lost during the reign of his son, Henry VI. The loss of the French possessions, together with the weak government of Henry VI, led to the outbreak of the Wars of the Roses, a campaign led by the supporters of Richard, Duke of York and Protector of England, during the illness of his cousin, Henry VI, to place Richard on the throne instead of Henry.

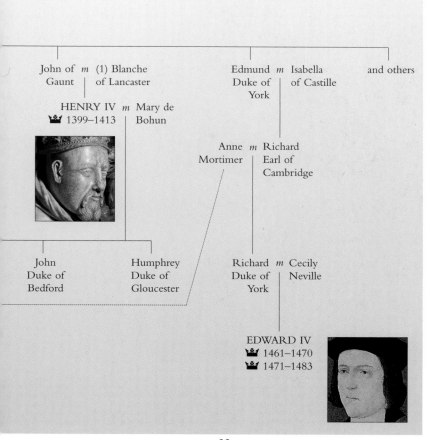

John of *m* (1) Blanche of Lancaster
Gaunt

Edmund *m* Isabella of Castille
Duke of York

and others

HENRY IV *m* Mary de Bohun
👑 1399–1413

Anne *m* Richard
Mortimer Earl of Cambridge

John Duke of Bedford

Humphrey Duke of Gloucester

Richard *m* Cecily Neville
Duke of York

EDWARD IV
👑 1461–1470
👑 1471–1483

HENRY IV

1399–1413

HENRY'S SEIZURE OF THE THRONE from Richard II was never questioned by Parliament, and indeed many people welcomed the accession of this strong and able ruler. However, throughout his reign, Henry was troubled by revolts against him by those who had once been his most loyal supporters.

♛ BIOGRAPHY

◆ **Born** 1367, fourth son of John of Gaunt and Blanche of Lancaster.
◆ **Married** Mary de Bohun, 1380/81, 7 children; Joan of Navarre, 7 Feb 1403.
◆ **Acceded** 30 Sept 1399.
◆ **Crowned** Westminster Abbey, 13 Oct 1399.
◆ **Died** 1413, aged 55.

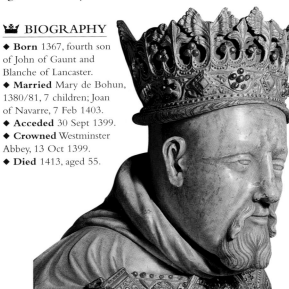

TROUBLED MAN
Worn down by conflict and financial problems, Henry IV died a shadow of his former, vigorous self. This gilt and painted effigy of Henry stands next to that of his second wife, Joan, above their tombs in Canterbury Cathedral.

EVENTS OF THE REIGN

◆ **1399** Henry returns from exile in France to reclaim his estates seized by Richard II; he claims the throne and is crowned. Richard is deposed and later imprisoned in Pontefract Castle.
◆ **1400** Richard dies from self-inflicted starvation.
◆ **1400** Death of the poet Geoffrey Chaucer.
◆ **1401–15** Owain Glyndwr leads Welsh revolt against English rule.

◆ **1401** Statute of *De heretico comburendo* – On the burning of heretics – leads to many Lollards, followers of John Wycliffe, being burned at the stake.
◆ **1402** State visit to England of Manuel II, the Byzantine emperor.
◆ **1403** First rebellion by the Percy family from Northumberland defeated at the Battle of Shrewsbury.
◆ **1404** Glyndwr makes a treaty with the French,

who send an army in 1405 to support the rebellion against the English.
◆ **1405** Second Percy rebellion takes place.
◆ **1406** Henry contracts a leprosy-like illness.
◆ **1408** Third Percy rebellion takes place.
◆ **1411–26** Construction of the London Guildhall.
◆ **1413** Henry dies at Westminster, worn out by constant revolts and shortage of money.

HENRY V

1413–1422

SOON AFTER SUCCEEDING HIS FATHER, Henry V revived the 100 Years' War with France. In 1415, Henry defeated the French army at Agincourt, and by 1420 he had forced the French King, Charles VI, to accept him as his heir. This pact was sealed by Henry's marriage to Charles's daughter, Catherine.

♛ BIOGRAPHY

- **Born** Monmouth Castle, 9 Aug or 16 Sept 1387, second son of Henry IV and Mary de Bohun.
- **Acceded** 21 Mar 1413.
- **Crowned** Westminster Abbey, 9 April 1413.
- **Married** Catherine of France, Troyes, France, 2/3 June 1420, 1 son.
- **Died** Vincennes Castle, France, 1 Sept 1422, aged 34 or 35.

CHIVALRIC KING
This portrait of Henry by an unknown artist shows a sensitive and thoughtful young man, although history recalls him as an adventurous, even headstrong, leader. As well as being a shrewd tactician, both militarily and politically, he was deeply religious and dealt mercifully with his enemies.

EVENTS OF THE REIGN

- **1413** Henry accedes to the throne at the age of 25 upon the death of his father, Henry IV.
- **1415** Henry thwarts the Cambridge plot, an attempt by a group of nobles to replace him on the throne with his cousin, Edmund Mortimer, Earl of March.
- **1415** Henry renews the war against France in order to win back territories lost by his ancestors. After a five-week siege, he captures Harfleur, the leading port in north-west France. A few weeks later he wins the Battle of Agincourt, at which 6,000 Frenchmen are killed, while less than 400 English soldiers lose their lives.
- **1416** Death of Owain Glyndwr, leader of the Welsh revolt.
- **1420** Under the Treaty of Troyes, Henry becomes Regent of France and heir to the French King, Charles VI.
- **1420** Henry marries Catherine, daughter of Charles VI.
- **1421** Birth of Prince Henry, later Henry VI.
- **1422** Henry V dies before he can succeed to the French throne. King Charles VI of France dies the following month, leaving Henry VI, Henry's 10-month-old son, as King of France and England.

HENRY VI

1422–1461, 1470–1471

ENRY VI ASCENDED to the thrones of England and France in 1422. During his long reign, his own mind failed him more than once and he had to submit the kingdom to the rule of a Protector, Richard, Duke of York. This led to civil war and his throne was taken away from him by the Protector's son, Edward IV, in 1461, given back briefly in 1470, and again taken away in 1471. Weeks later Henry was murdered in the Tower of London.

JOAN OF ARC

In 1422, Henry was king of a French people who had lost faith in their leaders and themselves. Their pride was restored by Joan of Arc, a young peasant girl from Domremy in eastern France. In 1429 Joan claimed to have had a vision from the Virgin Mary telling her to drive the English out of France, and she began a campaign that was to see the English expelled from all but Calais by 1453. In 1431 the English captured and burned Joan at the stake as a witch and heretic in Rouen.

THE WARS OF THE ROSES

The Wars of the Roses can be seen quite simply as the military expression of an on-going family quarrel between two branches of the royal house of Plantagenet, the houses of Lancaster and York. The wars broke out in 1455 as a result of Yorkist exasperation with the weak and inefficient government of Henry VI, and lasted, with lengthy intervals, for 30 years.

EVENTS OF THE REIGN 1422–1459

◆ **1422** Henry becomes King of England on the death of his father, Henry V, and then, two months later, King of France on the death of his grandfather, Charles VI.

◆ **1422** John, Duke of Bedford, is appointed Regent of France; Humphrey, Duke of Gloucester, becomes Regent of England.

◆ **1429** The young peasant girl Joan of Arc begins her campaign to expel the English from France.

◆ **1431** The English capture Joan of Arc. She is burned at the stake as a witch and heretic in Rouen on 30 May.

◆ **1437** Henry assumes personal rule of England.

◆ **1453** End of 100 Years' War. The English are driven out of France.

◆ **1454** Richard, Duke of York, is made Protector during Henry's illness.

◆ **1455** Duke of York is dismissed. York raises an army and defeats the King's Lancastrian forces at the Battle of St. Albans. The Lancastrian leader, the Duke of Somerset, is killed. York takes over the government of England.

◆ **1459** War is renewed and the Lancastrians are defeated at Bloreheath; the Yorkists are then defeated at Ludford. Parliament declares York a traitor.

👑 BIOGRAPHY

◆ **Born** Windsor Castle, 6 Dec 1421, son of Henry V and Catherine of France.
◆ **Acceded** 1 Sept 1422.
◆ **Crowned** Westminster Abbey, 5/6 Nov 1429.
◆ **Married** Margaret of Anjou, Titchfield Abbey, Hants, 23 April 1445, 1 son.
◆ **Deposed** 4 Mar 1461.
◆ **Restored** 30 Oct 1470.
◆ **Deposed** 11 Apr 1471.
◆ **Murdered** Tower of London, 27 May 1471, aged 49.

INGENUOUS KING

Gentle, kind, and extremely generous, Henry was a simple man, incapable of deceit or craftiness. Throughout his life, Henry was deeply religious, a trait that manifested itself in his great enthusiasm for education and building. This portrait of Henry, by an unknown artist, hangs in the library of Eton College.

EVENTS OF THE REIGN 1460–1471

◆ **1460** Yorkist army led by Richard Neville, Earl of Warwick, defeats Lancastrians at the Battle of Northampton. Henry VI is captured; his wife, Margaret, escapes to Scotland. Richard of York is again Protector.

◆ **1460** Margaret raises an army in the north and defeats and kills Richard of York at Wakefield.

◆ **1461** Henry is deposed by Richard's son Edward, Duke of York, who is then crowned Edward IV.

◆ **1462–3** Lancastrian revolts are suppressed.

◆ **1464** Warwick defeats Lancastrians at Battle of Hexham; Henry VI is captured and brought to the Tower of London.

◆ **1469–70** Warwick falls out with Edward IV, and defeats him at Edgecote. They are later reconciled but Warwick is banished. He makes peace with Margaret, returns to England with an army, and Edward flees to Flanders. Henry VI is restored to the throne.

◆ **1471** Edward returns to England and defeats and kills Warwick at the Battle of Barnet. Margaret is defeated at the Battle of Tewkesbury; her son Edward, Prince of Wales, is killed in battle.

◆ **1471** Henry is murdered in the Tower of London.

CHAPTER FIVE

THE HOUSE OF YORK

1461–1485

T HE HOUSE OF YORK had a stronger claim to the throne than the House of Lancaster, although both were branches of the House of Plantagenet. Edward IV was descended from two of Edward III's sons – Lionel of Clarence and Edmund of York.

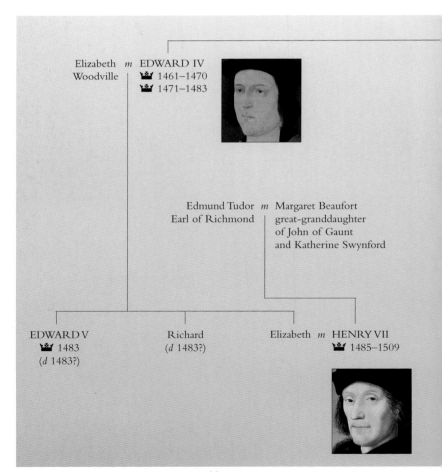

Elizabeth *m* EDWARD IV
Woodville   ♛ 1461–1470
                 ♛ 1471–1483

Edmund Tudor *m* Margaret Beaufort
Earl of Richmond   great-granddaughter
                     of John of Gaunt
                     and Katherine Swynford

EDWARD V   Richard   Elizabeth *m* HENRY VII
♛ 1483   (*d* 1483?)   ♛ 1485–1509
(*d* 1483?)

THE YORKIST DYNASTY

As the government of Henry VI became more inefficient, there was a growing clamour for Richard Plantagenet to govern the country. At first Henry's supporters resisted, but when the Queen gave birth to a son, Edward, in 1454, thus excluding Richard from the succession, the clamour mounted. Richard took up arms against the King and defeated a Lancastrian army at St. Albans in what was to be the first battle of the Wars of the Roses. In 1460 Richard formally claimed the throne but he was killed in battle at Wakefield. The following spring, his son Edward was proclaimed the first Yorkist king. The Yorkist dynasty only lasted until 1485, but in this time England enjoyed a leap forwards in national prosperity.

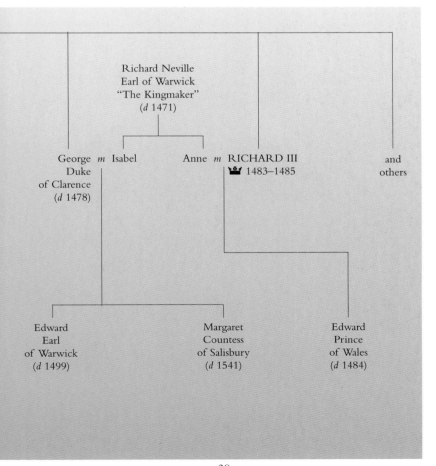

Richard Neville
Earl of Warwick
"The Kingmaker"
(*d* 1471)

George *m* Isabel   Anne *m* RICHARD III   and
Duke   1483–1485   others
of Clarence
(*d* 1478)

Edward   Margaret   Edward
Earl   Countess   Prince
of Warwick   of Salisbury   of Wales
(*d* 1499)   (*d* 1541)   (*d* 1484)

EDWARD IV

1461–1470, 1471–1483

EDWARD IV CAME TO THE THRONE with two aims: to restore the system of justice and to improve royal finances, both of which had suffered during the reign of Henry VI. Edward proved himself an able ruler, and during his reign, which was briefly interrupted, the country enjoyed a well-deserved period of peace.

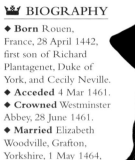

♔ BIOGRAPHY

- **Born** Rouen, France, 28 April 1442, first son of Richard Plantagenet, Duke of York, and Cecily Neville.
- **Acceded** 4 Mar 1461.
- **Crowned** Westminster Abbey, 28 June 1461.
- **Married** Elizabeth Woodville, Grafton, Yorkshire, 1 May 1464, 10 children.
- **Deposed** 3 Oct 1470.
- **Restored** 11 April 1471.
- **Died** Westminster, 9 April 1483, aged 40.

IMPOSING MAN
When Edward became King at the age of 18, he was described by many as a beautiful young man, about 2 metres (6 feet) tall, with polished manners and a genial disposition. The artist of this portrait of the King is unknown.

EVENTS OF THE REIGN

- **1461** Edward defeats the Lancastrian army at Mortimer's Cross and is proclaimed King by his cousin Warwick, "The Kingmaker", in succession to Henry VI.
- **1464** Edward marries Elizabeth Woodville, the widow of a commoner, offending Warwick.
- **1469** Warwick breaks with Edward and joins Henry VI's wife, Margaret, to usurp Edward.

- **1470** Edward is driven out of England to exile in Flanders when Henry VI is restored to the throne.
- **1471** Edward returns to England from Flanders and defeats and kills Warwick at the Battle of Barnet.
- **1471** Margaret is defeated at the Battle of Tewkesbury and the Lancasterian heir, Prince Edward, is killed. Soon after, Henry VI is murdered in the Tower of London.

- **1474** Edward grants privileges to the Hanseatic League of North German trading cities to conduct trade in England.
- **1476** William Caxton sets up a printing press in Westminster, London.
- **1478** Edward falls out with his brother George, Duke of Clarence, who is then murdered in the Tower, supposedly in a butt of malmsey wine.
- **1483** Death of Edward.

EDWARD V

1483

O N THE DEATH OF EDWARD IV in 1483, the crown passed to his young son, Edward V. But Edward was declared illegitimate and deposed in favour of his uncle, Richard. Edward and his younger brother were moved into the Tower of London, and after a few months the princes were never seen again.

👑 BIOGRAPHY

◆ **Born** Westminster Abbey Sanctuary, 1/2/4 Nov 1470, first son of Edward IV and Elizabeth Woodville.
◆ **Acceded** 9 April 1483.
◆ **Deposed** 25 June 1483.
◆ **Died** Sept 1483?, aged 12.

THE TWO PRINCES

This famous portrait of Edward and his younger brother Richard was painted by Sir John Everett Millais in the 19th century, some 400 years after their deaths. Very little is known about the character of Edward V. He was shielded from political life and saw little of his father.

EVENTS OF THE REIGN

◆ Edward V succeeds his father, Edward IV, in April and makes his way with his brother Richard from Ludlow Castle to London on 4 May. Edward IV's brother, Richard, Duke of Gloucester, is appointed Protector in Edward IV's will. Arrangements are made for Edward's coronation on 22 June.
◆ The two young princes lodge with the Bishop of London before moving to royal apartments in the Tower of London.
◆ In June Edward and Richard are declared illegitimate by Parliament. The Bishop of Bath and Wells reveals to the Protector that when Edward IV had married Elizabeth Woodville, he was already betrothed to Lady Eleanor Butler. As betrothal constituted the same commitment as marriage, Edward IV's marriage is invalid and his sons are illegitimate. Parliament meets and approves the proposal that Richard of Gloucester should succeed to the throne as Richard III.
◆ Last sighting of the two young princes in the grounds of the Tower of London in September. No one knows what happened to the princes, and their disappearance remains a mystery to this day.

RICHARD III

1483–1485

RICHARD III WAS KING FOR BARELY two years, but once he was dead, historians, clerics and even playwrights fell over themselves to blacken his name. Most of the propaganda was designed to serve the Tudor dynasty, which began when Henry VII's army defeated and killed Richard at the Battle of Bosworth in 1485. However, in more recent times, historians have questioned whether Richard III really deserves his evil reputation.

A MUCH-MALIGNED KING

Tall, lean, and with slender limbs, Richard was a handsome man. Contrary to William Shakespeare's portrayal of the King in *The Life and Death of King Richard III*, there is no evidence that Richard was a hunchback, although he might have had one shoulder slightly higher than the other. Devoted to his brother Edward, and reliable in all the many tasks Edward asked him to do, Richard was undoubtedly courageous and proved in his very short reign to be an energetic, painstaking, and just ruler.

THE BATTLE OF BOSWORTH

On 22 August 1485, the 8,000-strong army of Henry Tudor faced Richard's 12,000-strong army in fields just outside the town of Market Bosworth in Leicestershire. Richard's support soon ebbed away, but he himself dived courageously into the thick of battle, coming within a sword's length of Henry Tudor before he was cut down.

EVENTS OF THE REIGN 1483–1484

◆ **1483** Richard succeeds his brother Edward IV after confining his two nephews, Edward V and Richard, Duke of York, in the Tower of London; after a few months the two brothers are never seen again.

◆ **1483** The Duke of Buckingham is appointed Constable and Great Chamberlain of England.

◆ **1483** In October Richard crushes a rebellion led by his former supporter, the Duke of Buckingham. The rebellion was designed to put Henry Tudor, Earl of Richmond and sole surviving heir to the claims of the House of Lancaster, on the throne. Buckingham is captured, tried, and put to death.

◆ **1483** Foundation of the College of Arms.

◆ **1483** William Caxton prints Jacobus de Voragine's *Golden Legend*, a history of the saints.

◆ **1483** At the cathedral of Rheims, Henry Tudor swears a solemn oath to marry Elizabeth of York in the presence of the Lancastrian Court in exile.

◆ **1484** The Queen Dowager (widow of Edward IV) and her daughters leave the Sanctuary of Westminster and place themselves in Richard's care.

◆ **1484** Richard establishes his military headquarters

♛ BIOGRAPHY

◆ **Born** Fotheringhay Castle, Northants, 2 Oct 1452, third son of Richard Plantagenet, Duke of York, and Cecily Neville.
◆ **Married** Anne Neville, Westminster Abbey, 12 July 1472, 1 son.
◆ **Acceded** 26 June 1483.
◆ **Crowned** Westminster Abbey, 6 July 1483.
◆ **Died** Bosworth Field, Leicestershire, 22 Aug 1485, aged 32.

ENIGMATIC KING
Probably the most maligned of English kings, Richard III has stimulated more speculation and enquiry into his character than any other British monarch, either before or since.

EVENTS OF THE REIGN 1484–1485

behind the battlements of Nottingham Castle.
◆ **1484** Death of Richard's only son and heir, Edward, aged 9 years.
◆ **1484** Richard's heir apparent, John de la Pole, the Earl of Lincoln, is appointed Lord Lieutenant of Ireland.
◆ **1484** A Papal Bull is issued against witchcraft.
◆ **1484** Richard creates the Council of the North for better administration of the

North of England; it survives until its abolition by Parliament in 1641.
◆ **1484** Benevolences – compulsory gifts from individuals to the monarch – are abolished.
◆ **1484** Richard helps James III of Scotland to suppress a revolt by Albany.
◆ **1484** A bail system is introduced for defendants in court cases.
◆ **1484** Parliamentary statutes are written down

in English for the first time and printed.
◆ **1485** Death of Richard's wife, Queen Anne.
◆ **1485** Henry Tudor, Earl of Richmond, lands in West Wales in early August and gathers support as the Lancastrian claimant to the Yorkist-held throne.
◆ **1485** Richard is defeated and killed by Henry Tudor's army at Bosworth Field. The Wars of the Roses come to an end.

CHAPTER SIX

THE
TUDORS
1485–1603

THE ACCESSION OF HENRY as the first Tudor king marked the end of the Middle Ages. The Wars of the Roses had so weakened the nobility that the Tudors were able to wield far more power than their Plantagenet predecessors had done.

HENRY VII *m* Elizabeth of York
♚ 1485–1509 | (d 1503)

Arthur *m* (1) Catherine *m* HENRY VIII *m* (2) Anne *m* (3) Jane Seymour
Prince   of Aragon ♚ 1509–1547   Boleyn   (d 1537)
of Wales   (*div* 1533)   (d 1536)   (4) Anne of Cleves
(d 1502)   (*div* 1540)
                                                          (5) Catherine Howard
                                                          (d 1542)
                                                          (6) Catherine Parr
                                                          (d 1548)

Philip II *m* MARY I   ELIZABETH I   EDWARD VI
of Spain   ♚ 1553–1558   ♚ 1558–1603   ♚ 1547–1553

JAMES VI of Scotland ♚ 1567–1625
JAMES I of England ♚ 1603–1625

NATIONAL PRIDE

The five Tudor monarchs were not always popular – indeed in some instances they were detested – but none was either murdered or deposed. Curiously, the English people tolerated an absolutism that would have been unthinkable in the previous century. The Tudors did an enormous amount to generate national pride, chiefly by ensuring the involvement of far more sectors of the population in the development of national institutions and the growth of national aspirations. Henry VII stimulated a great increase in economic activity, favouring the merchant and manufacturing classes, and the whole period was illuminated by the flowering of the English Renaissance in architecture, literature, and the theatre.

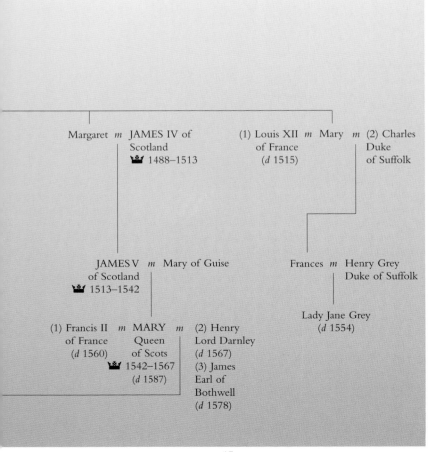

Margaret *m* JAMES IV of Scotland 👑 1488–1513

(1) Louis XII *m* Mary *m* (2) Charles
of France   Duke
(*d* 1515)   of Suffolk

JAMES V *m* Mary of Guise
of Scotland
👑 1513–1542

Frances *m* Henry Grey
Duke of Suffolk

Lady Jane Grey
(*d* 1554)

(1) Francis II *m* MARY *m* (2) Henry
of France   Queen   Lord Darnley
(*d* 1560)   of Scots   (*d* 1567)
👑 1542–1567   (3) James
(*d* 1587)   Earl of
Bothwell
(*d* 1578)

HENRY VII

1485–1509

ENRY ACCEDED TO THE THRONE after defeating Richard III at Bosworth in 1485. He broke the power of the barons by reviving the Court of Star Chamber to try the barons if they broke the law. He pursued peaceful, commercially orientated policies, ensuring a handsome credit for the royal exchequer.

♛ BIOGRAPHY

◆ **Born** Pembroke Castle, Wales, 28 Jan 1457, son of Edward Tudor and Margaret Beaufort.
◆ **Acceded** 22 Aug 1485.
◆ **Crowned** Westminster Abbey, 30 Oct 1485.
◆ **Married** Elizabeth of York, Westminster Abbey, 18 Jan 1486, 8 children.
◆ **Died** Richmond Palace, Surrey, 21 April 1509, aged 52.

ABLE MONARCH
Henry was tall, dark, blue-eyed, well-built, and athletic. He was interested in the arts, and skilled in diplomacy, as well as financially astute. This portrait by Michiel Sittow, painted in 1505, shows a man of reserved character.

EVENTS OF THE REIGN 1485–1509

◆ **1485** Henry accedes to the throne after defeating Richard III of York at the Battle of Bosworth.
◆ **1485** Henry forms the Yeomen of the Guard.
◆ **1486** Henry marries Elizabeth of York, thereby uniting the houses of York and Lancaster.
◆ **1487** Henry revives the Court of Star Chamber.
◆ **1487** Henry crushes a revolt by the Earl of Lincoln on behalf of

Lambert Simnel, a claimant to the throne, at Stoke.
◆ **1491** Henry invades France but at the Treaty of Etaples agrees to withdraw English forces in return for a large sum of money.
◆ **1492** Perkin Warbeck claims the throne and attempts to overthrow Henry, but is defeated and put to death in 1499.
◆ **1492** Christopher Columbus crosses Atlantic and discovers America.

◆ **1503** Prince Arthur, Henry's eldest son, dies, and Prince Henry (the future Henry VIII) becomes heir to the throne, later marrying Arthur's widow, Catherine of Aragon.
◆ **1503** Princess Margaret, Henry's daughter, marries James IV of Scotland.
◆ **1503** Death of Elizabeth of York, Henry's wife.
◆ **1509** Henry VII dies at Richmond Palace, at the age of 52.

HENRY VIII

1509–1547

I N THE EARLY YEARS of his reign, Henry was content to leave governing in the hands of his Chancellor, Cardinal Wolsey. However, Wolsey fell from power when he failed to secure a divorce for Henry from Catherine of Aragon. The King became increasingly autocratic and by his death he was much hated.

"KING HAL"

As a young man, Henry was tall and handsome. However, when older, he became grossly overweight and was riddled with disease.

♛ BIOGRAPHY

◆ **Born** Greenwich, 28 June 1491, second son of Henry VII and Elizabeth.
◆ **Acceded** 22 April 1509.
◆ **Crowned** Westminster Abbey, 24 June 1509.
◆ **Married** Six wives (*see page 49*).
◆ **Died** Whitehall, 28 Jan 1547, aged 55.

EVENTS OF THE REIGN 1509–1533

◆ **1509** Henry accedes to the throne on the death of his father, Henry VII.
◆ **1509** Henry marries Catherine of Aragon, daughter of the Spanish King and Queen, and widow of his elder brother, Arthur.
◆ **1513** The English defeat the Scots at the Battle of Flodden Field. James IV of Scotland is killed.
◆ **1515** Thomas Wolsey becomes Chancellor.

◆ **1516** Catherine gives birth to Princess Mary (later Mary I).
◆ **1517** Martin Luther publishes his 95 theses against the abuses of the Roman Catholic Church.
◆ **1518** The Pope and the Kings of England, France, and Spain pledge peace in Europe.
◆ **1520** Henry holds peace talks with Francis I of France at the Field of the Cloth of Gold.

◆ **1529** Cardinal Wolsey is accused of high treason, but dies before he can be brought to trial.
◆ **1529** Sir Thomas More becomes Chancellor.
◆ **1532** Sir Thomas More resigns from the Chancellorship.
◆ **1533** Henry's marriage to Catherine of Aragon is annulled by Archbishop Thomas Cranmer.
◆ **1533** Henry marries Anne Boleyn.

GOVERNING BY PROXY

Although well-educated, Henry at first had no enthusiasm for statecraft or personal rule, preferring hunting, the tourney, games, mistresses, and music to governing the country. During the first two decades of his reign, Henry entrusted the business of government to his great minister, Cardinal Thomas Wolsey. Born in 1475, Wolsey was the son of an Ipswich butcher. He entered the church and became Archbishop of York in 1514. A year later he received his cardinal's hat and became the Chancellor of England. Cardinal Wolsey looked after England's affairs at home and abroad with great skill, presiding over a period of growing prosperity. However, Wolsey fell from grace in 1529 when he failed to secure Henry's divorce from Catherine of Aragon. He died that year before he could be brought to trial for treason.

THE HANDSOME KING
This portrait of the King was painted by Hans Holbein.

DISSOLUTION OF THE MONASTERIES

After Henry VIII's break with Rome, Thomas Cromwell set up a commission to examine the state of every monastery and convent in England, with a view to possible closure and appropriation of its wealth by the Crown. Many were found to be racked with corruption. Henry, who urgently needed money to finance his extravagant lifestyle, ordered their dissolution. In 1537, the smaller monasteries were closed and their property confiscated. The remainder were similarly dealt with in 1539.

EVENTS OF THE REIGN 1533–1547

- ◆ **1533** Princess Elizabeth (later Elizabeth I) is born.
- ◆ **1533** The Pope excommunicates Henry.
- ◆ **1534** The Act of Supremacy is passed, establishing Henry as head of the Church of England.
- ◆ **1535** Sir Thomas More is executed after refusing to recognize Henry as Supreme Head of the Church of England.
- ◆ **1535** Thomas Cromwell is made Vicar-General.

- ◆ **1536** Anne Boleyn is executed and Henry marries Jane Seymour.
- ◆ **1536** The Act of Union between Wales and England.
- ◆ **1536** Thomas Cromwell begins the dissolution of the monasteries.
- ◆ **1536–7** Great northern rising, known as the Pilgrimage of Grace.
- ◆ **1537** Jane Seymour dies giving birth to Edward (later Edward VI).

- ◆ **1540** Henry marries Anne of Cleves in January but the marriage is annulled in July.
- ◆ **1540** Execution of Thomas Cromwell on a charge of treason.
- ◆ **1540** Henry marries Catherine Howard.
- ◆ **1542** Catherine Howard is executed for treason.
- ◆ **1543** Henry marries the twice-widowed Catherine Parr, his sixth and last wife.
- ◆ **1547** Henry VIII dies.

THE SIX WIVES OF HENRY VIII

HENRY VIII HOLDS THE RECORD as the most married of English kings. His first three marriages were love matches, fuelled by a fervent desire to produce a male heir. His subsequent three marriages were motivated more by the search for a suitable step-mother for his children.

CATHERINE OF ARAGON
Catherine was an attractive woman with red-brown hair, a pretty mouth, and lovely eyes.

ANNE OF CLEVES
Described by Henry as the "Mare of Flanders", Anne was dull, ugly, and spoke no English.

THE WIVES

◆ **Catherine of Aragon**
Catherine married Henry in 1509. She gave birth eight times, but only Mary (later Mary I) survived. Desperate for a male heir, Henry had the marriage annulled in 1533.

◆ **Anne Boleyn**
Anne was already pregnant with the future Elizabeth I when she married Henry in 1533. The King soon lost interest in Anne and in 1536, she was beheaded.

◆ **Jane Seymour**
Jane caught Henry's eye while she was a lady-in-waiting to Anne Boleyn. She married the King in 1536, and bore him a son (the future Edward VI), but died of childbirth complications.

◆ **Anne of Cleves**
The German princess, Anne of Cleves, undertook an arranged marriage with Henry in January 1540. The King, however, refused to consummate the marriage,

and the marriage was annulled in July.

◆ **Catherine Howard**
Catherine married Henry in 1540, but was executed two years later for adultery.

◆ **Catherine Parr**
Henry saw the twice-widowed Catherine Parr as an ideal stepmother to his children. Both expected few physical demands of each other. Catherine outlived Henry, marrying again shortly after his death.

EDWARD VI

1547–1553

EDWARD VI ASCENDED the throne at the age of nine in 1547, but because he was a minor the government was managed by two Protectors throughout his six-year reign – firstly the Duke of Somerset and later the Duke of Northumberland. In late 1552, Edward caught tuberculosis, and he died the following year.

♛ BIOGRAPHY

◆ **Born** Hampton Court Palace, Surrey, 12 Oct 1537, son of Henry VIII and Jane Seymour.
◆ **Acceded** 28 Jan 1547.
◆ **Crowned** Westminster Abbey, 20 Feb 1547.
◆ **Died** Greenwich Palace, 6 July 1553, aged 15.

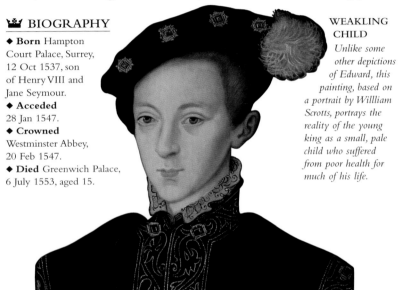

WEAKLING CHILD
Unlike some other depictions of Edward, this painting, based on a portrait by Willliam Scrotts, portrays the reality of the young king as a small, pale child who suffered from poor health for much of his life.

EVENTS OF THE REIGN

◆ **1547** Edward VI accedes to the throne at the age of nine after the death of his father, Henry VIII.
◆ **1547** Edward Seymour, Earl of Hertford, uncle of Edward VI, is invested as Duke of Somerset and Protector of England.
◆ **1547** The English army defeats the Scots at Pinkie Cleugh as part of an attempt to force a marriage between Mary, Queen of Scots, and Edward VI.

◆ **1549** The First Act of Uniformity is passed, making the Roman Catholic mass illegal. The clergy are ordered to remove icons and statues of the saints, and whitewash over wall paintings.
◆ **1549** The First Book of Common Prayer is introduced, which changes the Church service from Latin to English.
◆ **1550** The Duke of Somerset is deposed as

Protector of England, and is replaced by John Dudley, Earl of Warwick, who creates himself Duke of Northumberland.
◆ **1552** The Duke of Somerset is executed.
◆ **1553** The Duke of Northumberland persuades Edward to nominate Lady Jane Grey as his heir, in an attempt to secure the Protestant succession.
◆ **1553** Edward VI dies at Greenwich Palace.

MARY I

1553–1558

THE DAUGHTER OF HENRY VIII and Catherine of Aragon, Mary was, like her mother, a fervent Catholic. With public support, she deposed the interloper Lady Jane Grey. Mary had numerous Protestants burned at the stake for heresy, repealed Protestant legislation, and restored Papal supremacy in England.

♛ BIOGRAPHY

- **Born** Greenwich Palace, 18 Feb 1516, daughter of Henry VIII and Catherine of Aragon.
- **Acceded** 19 July 1553.
- **Crowned** Westminster Abbey, 1 Oct 1553.
- **Married** Philip of Spain, Winchester Cathedral, 25 July 1554.
- **Died** St. James's Palace, London, 17 Nov 1558, aged 42.

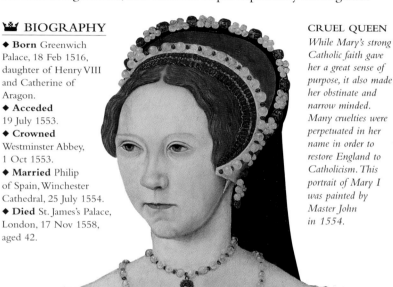

CRUEL QUEEN
While Mary's strong Catholic faith gave her a great sense of purpose, it also made her obstinate and narrow minded. Many cruelties were perpetuated in her name in order to restore England to Catholicism. This portrait of Mary I was painted by Master John in 1554.

EVENTS OF THE REIGN

- **1553** Lady Jane Grey is proclaimed Queen by the Protector, the Duke of Northumberland. After nine days, Mary arrives in London, Lady Jane Grey is arrested, and Mary is crowned Queen.
- **1554** After Mary declares her intention to marry Philip of Spain, Sir Thomas Wyatt leads a revolt to depose her.
- **1554** Wyatt's rebellion is crushed; Sir Thomas Wyatt, Lady Jane Grey, and her husband are executed.
- **1554** Mary marries Philip of Spain.
- **1554** The persecution of Protestants begins, the heresy laws are revived, and England is reconciled to Papal authority.
- **1555** Three Protestant bishops are burned at the stake for heresy.
- **1556** Cardinal Reginald Pole is appointed the Archbishop of Canterbury.
- **1556** Thomas Cranmer, former Archbishop of Canterbury, is burned at the stake for heresy.
- **1556** Philip becomes King of Spain; he leaves England, never to return.
- **1557** England declares war on France.
- **1558** Port of Calais – the last English possession in France – is captured by the French.
- **1558** Mary dies at St. James's Palace, London.

ELIZABETH I
1558–1603

DESPITE A TRAUMATIC EARLY LIFE, Elizabeth displayed strength and prudence as Queen, choosing loyal and able advisers. Throughout her 45-year reign, the "Virgin Queen" showed considerable political acumen in defying a largely Catholic Europe intent on overturning the Protestant faith, while presiding over a period of adventure that saw a vast expansion of English trade and prosperity and significant developments in the arts.

ROYAL FAVOURITES

Elizabeth spent her life surrounded by suitors including Philip II of Spain, Robert Dudley, Earl of Leicester, and Francis, Duke of Alençon, yet she never married. A shrewd observer commented: "The Queen would like everyone to be in love with her, but I doubt whether she will ever be in love with anyone enough to marry him".

THE SPANISH ARMADA

In 1588, 130 Spanish ships set sail to invade England. The English ships attacked the vastly superior Spanish force as it sailed up the Channel and anchored off Calais. The English then sent in fireships to break up the Spanish fleet, forcing it back into the Channel off Gravelines, where the decisive action was fought on 9 August. Battered by English guns, the Spanish retreated northwards, where severe Atlantic gales and the rocky coastline wrecked the majority of the surviving ships.

EVENTS OF THE REIGN 1558–1568

◆ **1558** Elizabeth accedes to the throne on the death of her half-sister, Mary.

◆ **1559** Elizabeth is crowned Queen of England at Westminster Abbey in January.

◆ **1559** Acts of Supremacy and Uniformity restore the Protestant Church in England and make Elizabeth Head of the Church of England.

◆ **1559** The Revised Prayer Book of Elizabeth I is issued. It is less extreme than its predecessors.

◆ **1560** Elizabeth founds the Westminster School.

◆ **1562** Hawkins and Drake make first slave-trading voyage to America.

◆ **1562** Elizabeth gives aid to the Protestant Huguenots in the French Wars of Religion.

◆ **1563** John Foxe's *The Book of Martyrs,* the story of religious persecution, is published in England.

◆ **1563–4** 17,000 die of the Plague in London.

◆ **1564** Peace made between England and France at Troyes.

◆ **1564** Introduction of horse-drawn coaches into Britain from Holland.

◆ **1566** Elizabeth forbids Parliament to discuss her marriage prospects.

◆ **1568** Mary, Queen of Scots, flees to England from Scotland and is imprisoned by Elizabeth.

♔ BIOGRAPHY

◆ **Born** Greenwich Palace, 7 Sept 1533, only daughter of Henry VIII and Anne Boleyn.
◆ **Acceded** 17 Nov 1558.
◆ **Crowned** Westminster Abbey, 15 Jan 1559.
◆ **Died** Richmond Palace, Surrey, 24 Mar 1603, aged 69.

VIRGIN QUEEN
This portrait of the Queen by Marcus Gheeraerts the Younger was painted in about 1592, when the Queen was nearly 60.

EVENTS OF THE REIGN 1569–1603

◆ **1570** The Pope excommunicates Queen Elizabeth from the Catholic Church.
◆ **1577–80** Francis Drake sails around the world in the *Golden Hind.*
◆ **1579** Francis, Duke of Alençon, secretly comes to England, to try and marry Elizabeth.
◆ **1586** Mary, Queen of Scots, is sent to trial.
◆ **1587** Mary, Queen of Scots, is executed at

Fotheringhay Castle on charges of treason.
◆ **1587** Drake attacks the Spanish fleet in Cadiz.
◆ **1588** The English navy and bad weather defeat the Spanish Armada.
◆ **1588** Robert Dudley, Earl of Leicester, and a favourite of Elizabeth, dies.
◆ **1590** Edmund Spencer's romantic poem, *The Faerie Queen,* is published.
◆ **1595–6** Sir Walter Raleigh makes his first

expedition to the South American continent.
◆ **1588** Earl of Essex leads an expedition to Ireland.
◆ **1601** Earl of Essex is executed for leading a revolt against Elizabeth.
◆ **1601** A Poor Law is passed introducing a poor relief rate on property owners.
◆ **1601** First performance of Shakespeare's *Hamlet.*
◆ **1603** Elizabeth I dies at Richmond Palace, Surrey.

CHAPTER SEVEN

THE
KINGS & QUEENS
OF SCOTLAND

843–1603

IN THE 840s, KENNETH MACALPIN, King of Dalriada, created a united country in the north of Scotland, and he is regarded as Scotland's first king. His descendant, Malcolm II, made further conquests, and ruled over a territory much the same as it is today.

WAR WITH ENGLAND

Time and again English kings cast their greedy eyes upon their northern neighbour, determined one way or another to take it over. The story of the Scots from the 11th to the 16th century is, in large measure, one of valiant struggle to preserve their fragile independence. This struggle was often waged by the kings, notably Robert Bruce and the first four Jameses, in the face of opposition from the greedy Scottish nobility. Yet, in the end, the union of the two countries came about not by war but through the peaceful succession of a Scottish king to the English throne in 1603.

ARTISTIC ACHIEVEMENT *The early Stewart kings presided over a period of artistic revival in Scotland. This painting of the court of King James I is by the Italian artist Pinturicchio.*

CONFLICT WITH ENGLAND

1034–1214

THE PERIOD BETWEEN the accession of Duncan I in 1034 and the death of William the Lyon in 1214 was marked by almost continual conflict with England as successive Scottish kings invaded their southern neighbour in an attempt to annex the most northern counties of England.

DAVID I
This illustration comes from the charter founding the abbey of Kelso. David I, who founded several abbeys, is shown with his grandson, Malcolm IV.

FEUDAL KING

One of the greatest of Scotland's early kings was David I. The youngest of Malcolm III's sons, David continued the practice of introducing feudalism into Scotland. Several powerful Norman families settled in Scotland, including the FitzAlans from Brittany, whose senior representative became the hereditary Steward of Scotland and took the name of Stewart.

EVENTS OF THE PERIOD

◆ **1034** Duncan I succeeds to the Scottish throne.
◆ **1040** Duncan is killed in a civil war. His cousin, Macbeth, succeeds.
◆ **1057** Macbeth is slain at the Battle of Lumphanan by Malcolm, son of Duncan I, who takes the throne as Malcolm III.
◆ **1072** Malcolm is forced to recognize William the Conqueror as overlord.
◆ **1093** Malcolm invades England but is killed. He is

succeeded by his brother Donald II (Donald Bane).
◆ **1094** Donald Bane is driven out by Duncan, Malcolm's III's son, who becomes Duncan II. He is killed a few months later and Donald Bane returns.
◆ **1097** Donald Bane is driven out again, this time by Edgar, half-brother of Duncan II.
◆ **1107** Edgar dies and is succeeded by his younger brother, Alexander I.

◆ **1124** Alexander dies and is succeeded by David I.
◆ **1154** David I dies and is succeeded by Malcolm IV.
◆ **1165** Malcolm IV dies and is succeeded by his brother, William the Lyon.
◆ **1173–4** William the Lyon invades England but is captured by Henry II and forced to surrender Scottish independence.
◆ **1189** Scotland is recognized as independent by Richard I of England.

TWO ALEXANDERS

1214–1305

WHEN ALEXANDER, the son of William the Lyon, came to the throne in 1214, he made it his priority to end the Viking occupation of the Western Isles and some areas of the Scottish mainland.

THWARTED EXPEDITION

In 1249 Alexander assembled a huge fleet of ships to invade the Western Isles, but on his way to join the fleet, he died, and the expedition was temporarily called off.

ALEXANDER III

His son, Alexander III, was only eight years old when he became king, and for a time Scotland was ruled by regents. In 1263, he finally expelled the Vikings from the Western Isles. He died in 1286, and by 1296 Scotland was under direct English rule. William Wallace led resistance against the English until his capture in 1305.

ROYAL SEAL
A strong ruler, Alexander II asserted control over most of present-day Scotland. His seal is shown above.

EVENTS OF THE PERIOD

- **1214** Accession of Alexander II, son of William the Lyon.
- **1217** Peace treaty with England guarantees peace for almost 20 years.
- **1237** Border between Scotland and England agreed by Treaty of York.
- **1249** Alexander launches an invasion of the Western Isles but dies before the expedition sets sail. He is succeeded by his son, Alexander III.

- **1263** Alexander III defeats Viking army at the Battle of Largs.
- **1286** Alexander dies in riding accident leaving the throne to his four-year-old granddaughter, Margaret.
- **1290** Margaret dies. Edward I of England is asked to select a successor.
- **1292** John Balliol is chosen to be King.
- **1295** Treaty between Scotland and France begins the "Auld Alliance".

- **1296** Edward I invades Scotland and deposes Balliol. Edward seizes the Stone of Scone – on which the Scottish Kings sit at their coronation – and takes it to London.
- **1297** William Wallace defeats English army at Stirling Bridge.
- **1305** Wallace is captured and taken to London, where he is tried for treason, and hanged, drawn, and quartered.

ROBERT BRUCE

1306–1329

I N 1306 ROBERT BRUCE was crowned king at Scone, an event that enraged the dying Edward I of England, who set out to invade Scotland. Bruce fled, and for several years remained in hiding. In 1314, Bruce defeated the English army at Bannockburn. This defeat did not, however, result in recognition of Scotland's independence. The fighting continued until 1328, when Edward III formally recognized Bruce as king of an independent Scotland.

BANNOCKBURN

In June 1314 Robert Bruce besieged Stirling Castle, which was held by the English. A huge army, sent by Edward II to relieve the castle, camped at Bannockburn, two miles to the south, and on 24 June the two armies met. Bruce's Scottish army was only one-third the size of the English army, but his soldiers managed to break the English lines. The English gave ground and fled from the field, the defeated Edward II among them.

THE DECLARATION OF ARBROATH

After Bannockburn, Bruce expected England to leave the country alone. This did not happen, and in 1320 a number of Scottish lords and bishops met in Arbroath and wrote to Pope John XXII insisting that he recognize Scotland's independence. "For as long as one hundred of us shall remain alive we shall never in any wise consent to submit to the rule of the English, for it is not for glory we fight... but for freedom alone."

EVENTS OF THE REIGN

◆ **1306** Robert Bruce is crowned king at Scone but is driven into hiding by the English occupation army of Edward I.

◆ **1307** Edward I sets out to invade Scotland but dies on his way north. Bruce begins campaign to drive the English out of Scotland.

◆ **1307** English forces defeated by Bruce at Loudon Hill.

◆ **1308** Bruce ravages the lands of the Earl of Buchan.

◆ **1309** The Douglases join forces with Bruce against England.

◆ **1310** The Scots recapture their towns held by the English.

◆ **1311** The Scots plunder the North of England.

◆ **1314** Bruce besieges Stirling Castle. An English army sent to break the siege is routed at the Battle of Bannockburn.

◆ **1315** Edward Bruce, Robert Bruce's brother,

accepts the crown of Ireland from the Irish lords.

◆ **1320** Declaration of Arbroath is signed by nearly all the lords and bishops in Scotland and is sent to the Pope.

◆ **1323** Truce between Bruce and Edward II fails to stop warfare between the two countries.

◆ **1327** Edward II is formally deposed by Parliament in favour of his son Edward III.

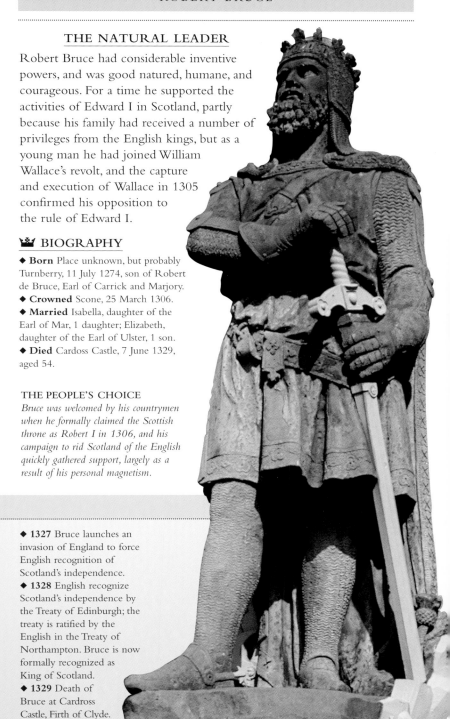

THE NATURAL LEADER

Robert Bruce had considerable inventive powers, and was good natured, humane, and courageous. For a time he supported the activities of Edward I in Scotland, partly because his family had received a number of privileges from the English kings, but as a young man he had joined William Wallace's revolt, and the capture and execution of Wallace in 1305 confirmed his opposition to the rule of Edward I.

♛ BIOGRAPHY

◆ **Born** Place unknown, but probably Turnberry, 11 July 1274, son of Robert de Bruce, Earl of Carrick and Marjory.
◆ **Crowned** Scone, 25 March 1306.
◆ **Married** Isabella, daughter of the Earl of Mar, 1 daughter; Elizabeth, daughter of the Earl of Ulster, 1 son.
◆ **Died** Cardoss Castle, 7 June 1329, aged 54.

THE PEOPLE'S CHOICE

Bruce was welcomed by his countrymen when he formally claimed the Scottish throne as Robert I in 1306, and his campaign to rid Scotland of the English quickly gathered support, largely as a result of his personal magnetism.

◆ **1327** Bruce launches an invasion of England to force English recognition of Scotland's independence.
◆ **1328** English recognize Scotland's independence by the Treaty of Edinburgh; the treaty is ratified by the English in the Treaty of Northampton. Bruce is now formally recognized as King of Scotland.
◆ **1329** Death of Bruce at Cardross Castle, Firth of Clyde.

"DARK & DRUBLIE DAYS"

1329–1406

THE REIGN OF DAVID II, son of Robert Bruce, was described as one of dark and troubled days. His successor, Robert, became the first Stewart king of Scotland, but he too was unable to give the country good government, and passed power over to his son, who eventually succeeded him as Robert III.

THE AULD ALLIANCE

In 1295, John Balliol, the Scottish King, signed a treaty with France, beginning the "Auld Alliance". For the next two centuries, Scotland looked to France for help in its conflicts with England, but help was not always forthcoming. The French were dismayed that the Scots preferred guerrilla warfare to open battle, and did not like the way they were expected to pay compensation for the damage their troops caused. Nevertheless, the Alliance held until the 1560s, when Scotland became Protestant.

ROBERT III

The reign of Robert III was characterized by violence and lawlessness. As one chronicler wrote in 1398, "there was no law in Scotland, but he who was stronger oppressed him who was weaker, and the whole realm was a den of thieves. ... justice ... lay in exile outwith the bounds of the kingdom". Even allowing for exaggeration, it was clearly a gloomy time.

EVENTS OF THE PERIOD 1329–1363

◆ **1329** David II succeeds to the Scottish throne on the death of his father, Robert Bruce.
◆ **1332** Edward Balliol, son of John Balliol, invades Scotland and forces David II into exile.
◆ **1333** Edward III of England invades Scotland and defeats the Scots at Halidon Hill. The English capture Berwick.
◆ **1337** The beginning of the 100 Years' War between

England and France diverts English attention away from Scotland.
◆ **1341** David II invades Scotland. Edward Balliol is expelled and David reclaims his throne.
◆ **1346** David II invades England to help the French King, who is under pressure from the English armies in France. David is defeated and captured at Neville's Cross. He is taken to the Tower of London, where he

is imprisoned for the next 11 years.
◆ **1348–50** Black Death affects parts of Scotland.
◆ **1357** By the Treaty of Berwick, David II is freed from prison and allowed to return home to Scotland on payment of a huge ransom.
◆ **1363** Unable to continue payments of the ransom, David returns to London and offers to bequeath the Scottish throne to Edward III or his heirs in return for a

PRISONER OF THE ENGLISH

In 1346, David II invaded England in support of his French allies but was defeated. He remained a prisoner in England until released in 1357 on payment of a huge ransom.

THE RANSOM

By 1363 the financial situation in Scotland was so bad that David went to London to negotiate a cancellation of the ransom payments if he bequeathed his throne to Edward III. The Scottish Parliament repudiated the proposal, preferring to bankrupt the country rather than lose its independence.

A KING'S RANSOM
David II offers Edward III of England the Scottish throne in return for his freedom.

EVENTS OF THE PERIOD 1363–1406

cancellation of the ransom, subject to approval of the Scottish Parliament.

◆ **1364** Scottish Parliament meets at Scone and refuses to approve David's deal with Edward III.

◆ **1371** Death of David II. He is succeeded by his nephew, Robert Stewart, the first Stewart King of Scotland. Robert, the hereditary High Steward of Scotland and grandson of Robert Bruce, is crowned

Robert II. A weak and ineffectual ruler, he hands over power to his eldest son John, Earl of Carrick.

◆ **1384** Truce is arranged between England, Scotland, and France. Scotland refuses to recognize truce; Anglo-Scottish war resumes.

◆ **1388** Scots defeat English at the Battle of Otterburn in the Borders.

◆ **1390** Robert II dies and is succeeded by his son John, who becomes

Robert III. He delegates power to his younger brother, the Earl of Fife, later the Duke of Albany.

◆ **1406** James, son of Robert III, is taken prisoner by pirates on his way from Scotland to France and is taken by ship to London, where Henry IV of England confines him in the Tower of London for 18 years. The news of James's capture brings on his father's premature death.

EARLY STEWARTS

1406–1513

THE 15TH CENTURY in Scotland is often depicted as an age of lawlessness, dominated by endless conflict between the Stewart kings and the nobility. It was also an age in which three out of the four kings were very powerful and dealt effectively with the dangers they faced.

JAMES I

James spent the first 18 years of his rule as a prisoner. On his return to Scotland, James determined to reform his country. His first parliament rectified abuses in taxation and in the justice system, and dealt severely with the factious Highland lords. His reforming policies made James many enemies, and he was assassinated in 1437.

AN AGE OF ART

An accomplished poet and musician, James I encouraged an artistic revival in Scotland. This portrait is by Pinturicchio.

EVENTS OF THE PERIOD

◆ **1406** James I, son of Robert III, hears of his succession to the throne while a prisoner of Henry IV. Scotland is ruled in his absence by his uncle, the Duke of Albany.

◆ **1424** James I returns to Scotland to take his throne.

◆ **1437** Assassination of James I. He is succeeded by his son, James II.

◆ **1455** James II finally overcomes the Black Douglas family.

◆ **1460** James II is killed by an exploding cannon at the siege of Roxburgh Castle. He is succeeded by his son, James III.

◆ **1472** Scotland acquires the Orkney and Shetland Islands from Norway.

◆ **1482** Berwick is finally lost to the English.

◆ **1488** Battle of Sauchieburn, and the assassination of James III. He is succeeded by his son, James IV.

◆ **1503** James IV marries Margaret Tudor, the daughter of Henry VII.

◆ **1507** First printing press in Scotland is set up by Andrew Myllar.

◆ **1513** James IV invades England to support his French allies after the English king, Henry VIII, invades France. James and most of the Scottish nobility and clergy are slaughtered by the English army at the Battle of Flodden Field.

LATER STEWARTS

1513–1603

J AMES V WAS ONLY 17 MONTHS old when he became King, but he proved to be a competent and fair ruler. His successor, Mary, was only one-week-old, and it perhaps would have been better for Scotland had she never been born. Her son, James VI, who also succeeded as an infant in 1567, proved to be quite unworthy of the former greatness of the Stewarts.

SCOTTISH REFORMATION

The Reformation in Scotland was both religious and political in nature. The movement began in the 1540s and turned Scotland from a Catholic into a Protestant nation in less than 20 years.

MARY, QUEEN OF SCOTS

In 1568 Mary fled to England. Her arrival presented the Protestant Elizabeth with a problem: Mary was Elizabeth's heir but she was also a Catholic. Yet, if she was returned to Scotland, she would be executed. Elizabeth confined Mary for 18 years and only reluctantly allowed her to be tried for treason and executed.

QUEEN OF SCOTS
Although endowed with considerable intellectual gifts, Mary was also hot-tempered, arrogant, and lacking in political judgement.

EVENTS OF THE PERIOD

- **1513** The infant James V becomes king.
- **1542** James invades England but is defeated at the Battle of Solway Moss and dies a few weeks later. His daughter, the one-week-old Mary, succeeds.
- **1558** Mary marries the French Dauphin in Paris.
- **1559** Mary becomes Queen of France when her husband becomes King.
- **1560** Reformation Parliament decides that

Scotland is to be a Protestant nation.
- **1560** François II dies and Mary returns to Scotland in 1561.
- **1565** Mary marries her cousin, Henry, Lord Darnley.
- **1566** Mary's Italian secretary, David Rizzio, is murdered.
- **1567** Darnley is murdered in an explosion. Mary is implicated, but nothing is proved.

- **1567** Mary marries the Earl of Bothwell.
- **1567** The Scottish lords force Mary to abdicate. She then flees to England, where she is imprisoned by Elizabeth I. Mary's son becomes king as James VI.
- **1587** Mary is executed at Fotheringhay Castle.
- **1603** Elizabeth I dies. James VI of Scotland becomes James I of England, Scotland, and Ireland, uniting the crowns.

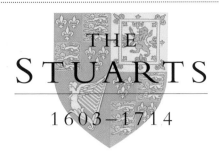

CHAPTER EIGHT

THE STUARTS
1603–1714

ELIZABETH I'S HEIR was James VI of Scotland, and in 1603 his accession united the crowns of England and Scotland. He was a Protestant but was tolerant of Catholics and allowed his heir, Charles, to be engaged to a French Catholic princess.

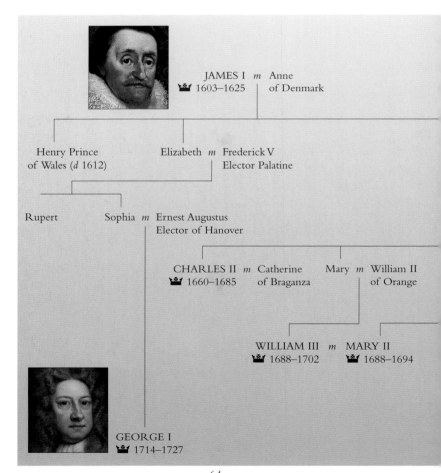

JAMES I *m* Anne
👑 1603–1625 | of Denmark

Henry Prince of Wales (*d* 1612)

Elizabeth *m* Frederick V
| Elector Palatine

Rupert

Sophia *m* Ernest Augustus
| Elector of Hanover

CHARLES II *m* Catherine
👑 1660–1685 | of Braganza

Mary *m* William II
| of Orange

WILLIAM III *m* MARY II
👑 1688–1702 👑 1688–1694

GEORGE I
👑 1714–1727

THE STUART KINGS

The next Stuart kings, Charles I and his son Charles II, although outwardly Protestant, more than tolerated Catholics, and James II converted to Catholicism. This association with the Church of Rome alarmed the predominantly Protestant population and was a major factor underlying the long-running conflict between king and Parliament. In the end, the 1701 Act of Settlement guaranteed that the country should never be ruled by a Catholic monarch. Another characteristic of the Stuart kings was their obsession with the doctrine of the Divine Right of Kings, by which kings were answerable not to man but to God. It is no small wonder that Parliament decided that a republican government was preferable.

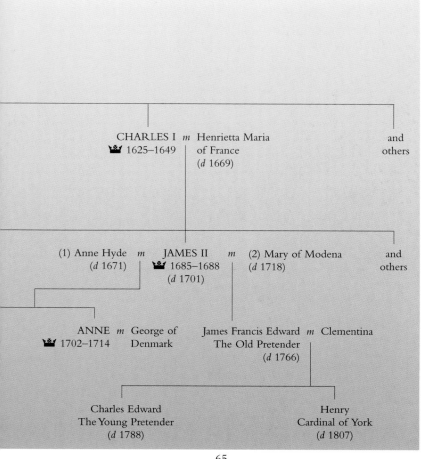

CHARLES I *m* Henrietta Maria   and
1625–1649   of France   others
(*d* 1669)

(1) Anne Hyde *m* JAMES II *m* (2) Mary of Modena   and
(*d* 1671)   1685–1688   (*d* 1718)   others
(*d* 1701)

ANNE *m* George of   James Francis Edward *m* Clementina
1702–1714   Denmark   The Old Pretender
(*d* 1766)

Charles Edward   Henry
The Young Pretender   Cardinal of York
(*d* 1788)   (*d* 1807)

JAMES I

1603–1625

WHEN JAMES ASCENDED the English throne in 1603, he had already been King of Scotland for 36 years. There, he had ruled by the Divine Right of Kings – whereby kings were appointed by God and so were not answerable to men. This style of government was unacceptable in England, so he ruled for long periods without Parliament. He thus squandered the legacy of strong government left to him by Elizabeth I.

THE KING'S FAVOURITES

The two principal favourites of James I were, in succession, Robert Ker and George Villiers. Ker, Earl of Somerset, was entrusted with the King's most intimate business. He angered the nation by encouraging the King to make an alliance with Spain, and by helping to raise dubious taxes. By 1616 the King had taken to Villiers, who became Earl of Buckingham.

THE GUNPOWDER PLOT

The Gunpowder Plot was hatched by conspirators disgruntled with the King's failure to grant toleration of Catholics. They planned to blow up the House of Lords when the King came for the opening of Parliament on 5 November 1605. They dug a tunnel under the House of Lords and filled a cellar with barrels of gunpowder. However, the plot was foiled when one of the conspirators, Guy Fawkes, was discovered in the cellar with the gunpowder. The conspirators were arrested, tried, and executed.

EVENTS OF THE REIGN 1603–1607

- ◆ **1603** James VI of Scotland becomes King James I of England, Scotland, and Ireland after the death of Elizabeth I.
- ◆ **1603** The Millenary Petition is presented to James I. It expresses Puritan desires for reforms to the Church of England.
- ◆ **1603** Plot against James I to set Arabella Stuart on the English throne. Sir Walter Raleigh is implicated and imprisoned.

- ◆ **1604** The Somerset House Peace Conference results in peace between England and Spain.
- ◆ **1604** The Hampton Court Conference fails to settle the doctrinal differences between the Anglican Church and its Puritan critics.
- ◆ **1604** Silk manufacturing begins in England.
- ◆ **1605** The Gunpowder Plot attempts to blow up King and Parliament.

- ◆ **1605** Shakespeare writes the tragedy, *King Lear*.
- ◆ **1606** The Gunpowder plotters are executed.
- ◆ **1607** The Earls of Tyrone and Tyrconnel end their rebellion against English rule of Ireland and flee to Europe; Ulster is colonized by Protestant settlers from Scotland and England.
- ◆ **1607** The English Parliament rejects Union with Scotland.

👑 BIOGRAPHY

◆ **Born** Edinburgh, 19 June 1566, son of
Mary, Queen of Scots and Lord Darnley.
◆ **Acceded** 24 Mar 1603.
◆ **Married** Anne of Denmark,
Oslo, 23 Nov 1589, 9 children.
◆ **Crowned** Westminster
Abbey, 25 July 1603.
◆ **Died** Hertfordshire,
27 Mar 1625, aged 58.

THE "WISEST FOOL"
*Although well educated,
James appeared foolish,
and was known as
the "wisest fool in
Christendom". This
portrait by Daniel
Mytens was
painted in 1621,
four years before
the King's death.*

EVENTS OF THE REIGN 1607–1625

◆ **1607** Common citizenship of English and Scottish persons is granted to those born after the accession of James VI of Scotland to the English throne.
◆ **1609** Shakespeare completes the *Sonnets*.
◆ **1611** Authorized Version of the Bible is published.
◆ **1611** Dissolution of the first Parliament of James I.
◆ **1611** Imprisonment of Arabella Stuart.

◆ **1612** Henry, Prince of Wales, dies of typhoid. His younger brother, Charles, becomes heir to the throne.
◆ **1612** Heretics are burned at the stake for the last time in England.
◆ **1613** Robert Ker is created Earl of Somerset.
◆ **1614** Second Parliament of James I meets.
◆ **1615** George Villiers becomes James's favourite.
◆ **1616** Playwright William Shakespeare dies.

◆ **1616** Raleigh is released from prison to lead an expedition to Guiana in search of El Dorado.
◆ **1617** George Villiers becomes the Earl of Buckingham.
◆ **1618** Raleigh is executed for alleged treason at Westminster.
◆ **1620** The Pilgrim Fathers set sail for America in the *Mayflower*.
◆ **1625** Death of James I, aged 58.

CHARLES I

1625–1649

THE SECOND SON OF JAMES I, Charles never expected to be King, only becoming heir to the throne after the death of his older brother, Henry, in 1612. Charles inherited his father's belief in the Divine Right of Kings and never wavered from that doctrine, even though it caused his own death. As a result, he was obstinate in his political dealings and constantly quarrelled with his parliaments, ruling without one for 11 years.

ABSOLUTE RULE

For more than a decade, Charles attempted to rule without Parliament, enforcing the royal prerogative through the Court of Star Chamber and the Court of High Commission. Charles gave these courts arbitrary powers to suppress political and religious opposition to his personal rule. The rivalry between Parliament and the monarchy gave rise to the Civil War, one of the greatest upheavals in British history.

BATTLE OF NASEBY

The major battle of the Civil War took place outside the town of Naseby in Northamptonshire on 14 June 1645. The 15,000-strong Parliamentary New Model Army, an untried force trained by Oliver Cromwell and led by Cromwell and Thomas Fairfax, faced a Royalist army half its size led by the King. The defeat of the Royalist army was decisive in giving victory to Parliament in the Civil War.

EVENTS OF THE REIGN

◆ **1625** Charles I succeeds his father, James I.

◆ **1626** Parliament attempts to impeach the Duke of Buckingham and is dissolved by Charles.

◆ **1627** England goes to war with France, but at La Rochelle the Duke of Buckingham fails to relieve the besieged Huguenots.

◆ **1628** The Petition of Right – a declaration of the "rights and liberties of the subject" – is

presented to the King, who agrees to it under protest.

◆ **1629** Charles dissolves Parliament and rules by himself until 1640.

◆ **1637** Charles tries to force new prayer book on Scots, who resist by signing the National Covenant.

◆ **1640** Charles summons the Short Parliament, which lasts for three weeks.

◆ **1640** Long Parliament summoned, which lasts until 1660.

◆ **1641** Abolition of the Star Chamber and Court of High Commission.

◆ **1642** Charles fails in his attempt to arrest five MPs.

◆ **1642** Outbreak of Civil War. The Royalists defeat the Parliamentary army at the Battle of Edgehill.

◆ **1643** Royalists defeat Parliamentary army at Chalgrove Field. Further battles result in stalemate.

◆ **1644** Royalists defeated at Marston Moor.

THE DEATH OF CHARLES

In early 1649, Parliament took the decision to try the King for waging war against his kingdom and against Parliament. The trial began on 20 January in Westminster Hall and was held in front of about 50 Members of Parliament. Throughout the trial, Charles stubbornly refused to recognize the legality of the court. On 27 January he was found guilty and sentenced to death by execution. The sentence was carried out on 30 January.

♛ BIOGRAPHY

◆ **Born** Dunfermline Palace, Fife, 19 Nov 1600, second son of James I and Anne of Denmark.
◆ **Acceded** 27 Mar 1625.
◆ **Married** Henrietta Maria of France, Canterbury, 13 June 1625, 9 children.
◆ **Crowned** Westminster Abbey, 2 Feb 1626.
◆ **Executed** 30 Jan 1649, aged 48.

THE KING'S CHARACTER

Shy and serious, Charles was a strange mixture of great personal charm, modesty, and politeness, combined with a lot of nervous tension and no self-confidence.

◆ **1645** Parliament creates New Model Army, which crushes the Royalist army at Naseby on 16 June.
◆ **1646** Charles surrenders to the Scots, who hand him over to Parliament.
◆ **1646–8** Negotiations take place between King and Parliament. King conspires with Scots to invade England on his behalf.
◆ **1648** The Scots are defeated at Preston.
◆ **1649** Charles is executed.

CHARLES II

1660–1685

C HARLES DID NOT ASCEND the English throne until the restoration of the monarchy in 1660. He divided his time between devious diplomatic activity, centred on getting as much financial support as he could from the Catholic Louis XIV of France, and a full and sensuous life devoted to his own pleasure.

♛ BIOGRAPHY

◆ **Born** St. James's Palace, 29 May 1630, eldest son of Charles I and Henrietta Maria.
◆ **Acceded** 29 May 1660.
◆ **Crowned** Westminster Abbey, 23 April 1661.
◆ **Married** Catherine of Braganza, Portsmouth, 21 May 1662.
◆ **Died** Whitehall, 6 Feb 1685, aged 54.

LADYKILLER

Tall and dark, with long, curly black hair, sparkling eyes, and a sensuous mouth, Charles was very attractive to women. Sir Godfrey Kneller painted this portrait in the early 1680s, near the end of Charles's reign.

EVENTS OF THE REIGN

◆ **1660** Charles returns to England from Holland and is restored to the throne.
◆ **1662** Act of Uniformity compels Puritans to accept the doctrines of the Church of England or leave the church.
◆ **1665–7** Outbreak of the Second Anglo-Dutch War.
◆ **1665** The Great Plague strikes London.
◆ **1666** The Great Fire of London rages for four days and three nights.

◆ **1667** The Earl of Clarendon is replaced by a five-man Cabal.
◆ **1670** Secret Treaty of Dover, by which Charles agrees to declare himself a Catholic and restore Catholicism in England in return for secret subsidies from Louis XIV of France.
◆ **1672–4** Outbreak of the Third Dutch War.
◆ **1673** Test Act keeps Roman Catholics out of political office.

◆ **1678** The Popish Plot is fabricated by Titus Oates. He alleges a Catholic plot to murder the King and restore Catholicism. The Government over-reacts, and many Catholic subjects are persecuted.
◆ **1679–81** Exclusion Bill attempts to exclude James, Charles's Catholic brother, from the succession.
◆ **1685** Charles is received into the Roman Catholic Church on his deathbed.

JAMES II

1685–1688

J AMES ASCENDED THE THRONE on the death of his brother, Charles II, in 1685. His intention of restoring Catholicism, and his policies, led to conflict with Church and Parliament. The birth of a son, and potential Catholic monarch, in 1688 intensified the conflict, and within six months he was forced to flee into exile.

♛ BIOGRAPHY

- **Born** St. James's Palace, 24 Oct 1633, second son of Charles I and Henrietta Maria.
- **Married** Anne Hyde, London, 3 Sept 1660, 8 children; Mary of Modena, Dover, Kent, 21 Nov 1673, 11 children.
- **Acceded** 6 Feb 1685.
- **Crowned** Westminster Abbey, 23 April 1685.
- **Deposed** 23 Dec 1688.
- **Died** France, 16 Sept 1701, aged 77.

KING TO BE
This portrait of James before he became king was completed in 1685 by Sir Godfrey Kneller.

EVENTS OF THE REIGN

- **1685** James succeeds his brother, Charles II.
- **1685** Rebellion of the Earl of Argyll in Scotland – designed to place the Duke of Monmouth, Charles II's illegitimate son, on the throne – is crushed and Argyll is executed.
- **1685** The Duke of Monmouth rebels against James, but is defeated at the Battle of Sedgmoor.
- **1685** Edict of Nantes – allowing freedom of religion to Huguenot Protestants – is revoked in France, resulting in thousands of Huguenot craftworkers and traders settling in England.
- **1686** James takes first measures to restore Catholicism in England, and sets up a standing army of 13,000 troops at Hounslow to overawe nearby London.
- **1688** Declaration of Indulgence suspends all laws against Catholics and Non-Conformists.
- **1688** James's wife, Mary of Modena, gives birth to a son and Catholic heir.
- **1688** Seven leading statesmen invite William of Orange, son-in-law of James, to England to restore English liberties.
- **1688** William of Orange lands at Torbay and advances on London.
- **1688** James abdicates and flees to exile in France.

WILLIAM & MARY

1689–1702

WHEN WILLIAM OF ORANGE was invited over to Britain to replace James II, it was arranged that he should rule jointly with his wife Mary, daughter of James. This unique arrangement lasted until the death of Mary in 1694, after which date William ruled by himself until his death in 1702.

♛ BIOGRAPHY

◆ **Born** *William:* The Hague, Holland, 14 Nov 1650, son of William of Nassau and Mary Stuart. *Mary:* St. James's Palace, 30 April 1662, daughter of James II and Anne Hyde.
◆ **Married** London, 4 Nov 1677.
◆ **Acceded** Jointly, 13 Feb 1689.
◆ **Crowned** Jointly, Westminster Abbey, 11 April 1689.
◆ **Died** Kensington Palace, *William:* 8 March 1702, aged 51. *Mary:* 28 Dec 1694, aged 32.

EVENTS OF THE REIGN

◆ **1689** Parliament draws up the Declaration of Right detailing the unconstitutional acts of James II. William and Mary become joint sovereigns.
◆ **1689** Bill of Rights is passed in Parliament.
◆ **1689** Catholic forces loyal to James II land in Ireland from France and lay siege to Londonderry.
◆ **1690** William defeats James at the Battle of the Boyne in Ireland.

◆ **1691** The Treaty of Limerick allows Catholics in Ireland to exercise their religion freely, but severe penal laws soon follow.
◆ **1691** French war begins.
◆ **1692** Glencoe Massacre.
◆ **1694** Death of Mary; William now rules alone.
◆ **1697** Peace of Ryswick ends the war with France.
◆ **1701** The Act of Settlement establishes Hanoverian and Protestant succession to the throne.

◆ **1701** James II dies in exile in France. French king recognizes James II's son as "James III".
◆ **1701** William forms grand alliance between England, Holland, and Austria to prevent the union of the French and Spanish crowns.
◆ **1701** War of the Spanish Succession breaks out in Europe over vacant throne.
◆ **1702** William dies after a riding accident.

ANNE

1702–1714

THE LAST STUART MONARCH, Queen Anne succeeded William of Orange in 1702. Shortly after Anne's accession, England declared war on France in the War of the Spanish Succession. In the course of this conflict Britain gained four great victories in battle, and established itself as a major European power.

♛ BIOGRAPHY

◆ **Born** St. James's Palace, 6 Feb 1665, the second daughter of James II and Anne Hyde.
◆ **Married** George, Prince of Denmark, St. James's Palace, 28 July 1683, 18 children.
◆ **Acceded** 8 March 1702.
◆ **Crowned** Westminster Abbey, 23 April 1702.
◆ **Died** Kensington Palace, 1 Aug 1714, aged 49.

QUEEN-TO-BE
This portrait of Anne, attributed to Sir Godfrey Kneller, was painted in about 1690, when she was 25 years old. In her youth Anne was not unattractive, although her short sightedness gave her a disconcerting squint. However, by the time she came to the throne, at the age of 35, she was plump.

EVENTS OF THE REIGN

◆ **1702** Anne succeeds her brother-in-law, William III.
◆ **1702** England declares war on France in the War of the Spanish Succession.
◆ **1704** English, Bavarian, and Austrian troops under Marlborough defeat the French at the Battle of Blenheim and save Austria from invasion.
◆ **1704** British capture Gibraltar from Spain.
◆ **1706** Marlborough defeats the French at the Battle of Ramillies, and expels the French from the Netherlands.
◆ **1707** The Act of Union unites the kingdoms of England and Scotland and transfers the seat of Scottish government to London.
◆ **1708** Marlborough defeats the French at the Battle of Oudenarde. The French incur heavy losses.
◆ **1708** Anne vetoes a parliamentary bill to reorganize the Scottish militia, the last time a bill is vetoed by the sovereign.
◆ **1709** Marlborough defeats the French at the Battle of Malplaquet.
◆ **1710** The Whig government falls and a Tory ministry is formed.
◆ **1713** The Treaty of Utrecht is signed by Britain and France, bringing to an end the War of the Spanish Succession.
◆ **1714** Queen Anne dies at Kensington Palace.

CHAPTER NINE

THE
HANOVERIANS
1714–1910

S UCCESSION WAS SETTLED upon the Protestant Electress of
Hanover, Sophia, granddaughter of James I, in 1701. When
she died in 1714, the succession passed to her son, George,
and on the death of Anne he became the first Hanoverian king.

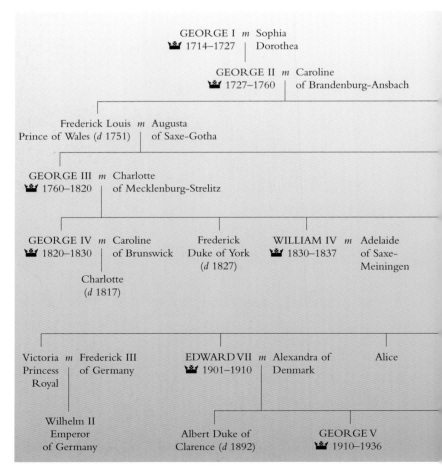

GEORGE I   *m*   Sophia
👑 1714–1727 | Dorothea

GEORGE II   *m*   Caroline
👑 1727–1760 | of Brandenburg-Ansbach

Frederick Louis   *m*   Augusta
Prince of Wales (*d* 1751) | of Saxe-Gotha

GEORGE III   *m*   Charlotte
👑 1760–1820 | of Mecklenburg-Strelitz

GEORGE IV   *m*   Caroline   Frederick   WILLIAM IV   *m*   Adelaide
👑 1820–1830 | of Brunswick   Duke of York   👑 1830–1837 | of Saxe-
    (*d* 1827)   Meiningen

Charlotte
(*d* 1817)

Victoria   *m*   Frederick III   EDWARD VII   *m*   Alexandra of   Alice
Princess | of Germany   👑 1901–1910 | Denmark
Royal

Wilhelm II   Albert Duke of   GEORGE V
Emperor   Clarence (*d* 1892)   👑 1910–1936
of Germany

THE NEW MONARCHS

To begin with, the Hanoverian kings had little going for them in Britain. George could speak no English and knew little of his new kingdom. Although the English Protestant majority approved of the Act of Settlement, which ensured a Protestant monarch, they wished Queen Anne's successor could have been more congenial. The minority who still preferred the Jacobite cause were influential and vociferous, and caused difficulties for the new dynasty for more than 30 years. Despite these problems, the Hanoverians worked hard to make themselves adaptable and to learn British ways. By the end of Queen Victoria's reign, the monarchy had surrendered most of its power, but retained influence and enjoyed great popularity.

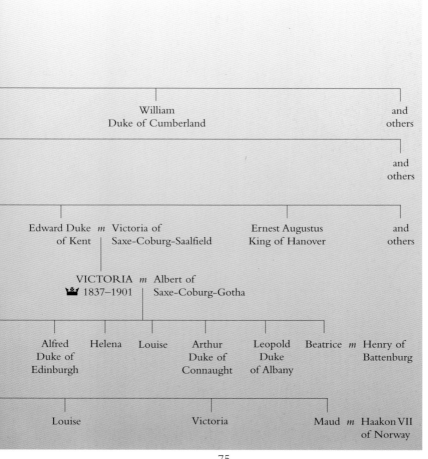

GEORGE I

1714–1727

EORGE I ARRIVED in England from Hanover unable to speak English and with a limited knowledge of Britain. Within a year he had to face a Jacobite rising in Scotland. It was only after 1721 that firm government was established when Robert Walpole became, in effect, Britain's first Prime Minister.

♕ BIOGRAPHY

◆ **Born** Osnabrück, Hanover, 7 June 1660, son of Ernest Augustus, Elector of Hanover.
◆ **Married** Sophia Dorothea, Germany, 21 Nov 1682, 2 children.
◆ **Acceded** 1 Aug 1714.
◆ **Crowned** Westminster Abbey, 20 Oct 1714.
◆ **Died** Hanover, 11 June 1727, aged 67.

GERMAN KING
This portrait of George I is from the studio of Sir Godfrey Kneller and was painted in 1714.

EVENTS OF THE REIGN

◆ **1714** George I, the first Hanoverian King, succeeds his distant cousin, Anne.
◆ **1714** A new Parliament is elected with a strong Whig majority, led by Charles Townshend and Robert Walpole.
◆ **1715** The Jacobite Rising begins in Scotland to place the "Old Pretender" – James Edward Stuart, heir to James II – on the throne. The rebellion is easily defeated.

◆ **1716** The Septennial Act allows for General Elections to be held every seven years.
◆ **1717** Townshend is dismissed from the government by George, causing Walpole to resign.
◆ **1719** Defoe publishes *Robinson Crusoe*.
◆ **1720** South Sea Bubble bursts, leaving many investors ruined.
◆ **1721** Sir Robert Walpole returns to government as

First Lord of the Treasury, where he remains in office until 1742; he is effectively the first Prime Minister.
◆ **1722** Death of the Duke of Marlborough.
◆ **1726** First circulating library in Britain opens in Edinburgh, Scotland.
◆ **1726** Jonathan Swift publishes *Gulliver's Travels*.
◆ **1727** Death of the scientist, Isaac Newton.
◆ **1727** George I dies in Hanover, aged 67.

GEORGE II

1727–1760

Although the first 12 years of George II's reign were peaceful, Britain was involved in almost continuous conflict in Europe after 1739. However, by the time of George's death in 1760, Britain was on its way to becoming a world power, with expansion in North America and India.

♛ BIOGRAPHY

◆ **Born** Hanover, 9 Nov 1683, son of George I and Sophia Dorothea.
◆ **Married** Caroline of Brandenburg-Ansbach, Hanover, 2 Sept 1705, 10 children.
◆ **Acceded** 11 June 1727.
◆ **Crowned** Westminster Abbey, 11 Oct 1727.
◆ **Died** Kensington Palace, 25 Oct 1760, aged 76.

WAR LEADER
Depicted here in the year of his coronation, George II later became the last British king to lead an army in the field, at the Battle of Dettingen.

EVENTS OF THE REIGN

◆ **1727** George succeeds his father, George I.
◆ **1732** A royal charter is granted for the founding of Georgia in America.
◆ **1737** Death of George's wife, Queen Caroline.
◆ **1738** John and Charles Wesley start the Methodist movement in Britain.
◆ **1739** Britain goes to war with Spain over Captain Jenkins's ear, claimed to have been cut off in a skirmish at sea.

◆ **1740–48** The War of Austrian Succession breaks out in Europe.
◆ **1742** Walpole resigns as Prime Minister.
◆ **1743** George leads troops into battle at Dettingen in Bavaria.
◆ **1745** Jacobite Rising in Scotland: Scottish victory at Prestonpans.
◆ **1746** Scots crushed at the Battle of Culloden.
◆ **1751** Death of Frederick, Prince of Wales;

his son, George, becomes heir to the throne.
◆ **1756** Britain declares war against France. Start of the Seven Years' War.
◆ **1757** Robert Clive wins the Battle of Plassey and secures the Indian province of Bengal for Britain.
◆ **1757** William Pitt becomes Prime Minister.
◆ **1759** Wolfe captures Quebec and expels the French from Canada.
◆ **1760** George II dies.

GEORGE III

1760–1820

THE FIRST HANOVERIAN MONARCH to be born and bred in England, George III was a conscientious ruler who believed in personal rule, albeit through constitutional means. His ability to speak to ordinary people earned him respect and popularity. From 1788, George suffered from porphyria, which made him appear deranged. By 1811 his health was so bad that his son was made Prince Regent until his father's death in 1820.

EARLY POLITICS

The early years of George's reign were difficult. George's first Prime Minister, Bute, was so unpopular that he was soon forced to resign. He was followed by a succession of ministers who failed to please either the King or Parliament. In 1770 George chose Lord North, a man who did what George requested and managed to appease Parliament.

UNFIT TO RULE

In 1788, 1801, and 1804 George III suffered a series of incapacitating fits that had all the appearance of progressively worsening mental illness. Although he recovered from these early attacks, in 1810 he had a relapse, after which he descended into permanent derangement and blindness for the last nine years of his life. Medical science has since discovered that George was suffering from an hereditary physical illness known as porphyria, in which the victim displays symptoms of delirium.

EVENTS OF THE REIGN 1760–1789

- **1760** George becomes king on the death of his grandfather, George II.
- **1762** The Earl of Bute is appointed Prime Minister. Bute proves so unpopular that he needs to have a bodyguard.
- **1763** Peace of Paris ends the Seven Years' War.
- **1765** Stamp Act raises taxes in American colonies.
- **1769–70** Captain James Cook's first voyage to explore the Pacific.

- **1770–82** Lord North serves as Prime Minister.
- **1771** *Encyclopedia Britannica* is first published.
- **1773** Boston Tea Party.
- **1773** The world's first cast-iron bridge is constructed over the River Severn at Coalbrookdale.
- **1775** American War of Independence begins when colonists fight British troops at Lexington.
- **1775** James Watt develops the steam engine.

- **1776** On 4 July, the American Congress passes the Declaration of Independence.
- **1782** Ireland obtains a short-lived parliament.
- **1783** Britain recognizes US independence.
- **1783–1801** William Pitt the Younger serves as Prime Minister.
- **1788** George suffers his first attack of porphyria.
- **1789** Outbreak of the French Revolution.

☙ BIOGRAPHY

◆ **Born** Norfolk House, London, 4 June 1738, son of Frederick, Prince of Wales, and Augusta of Saxe-Gotha-Altenburg.
◆ **Acceded** 25 Oct 1760.
◆ **Married** Charlotte of Mecklenburg-Strelitz, St. James's Palace, 8 Sept 1761, 15 children.
◆ **Crowned** Westminster Abbey, 21 Sept 1761.
◆ **Died** Windsor Castle, 29 Jan 1820, aged 81.

THE "MAD" KING
This portrait of the King was painted in the studio of Allan Ramsay in 1767, when George was 29 years old.

EVENTS OF THE REIGN 1790–1820

◆ **1791** Publication of James Boswell's *Life of Johnson* and Thomas Paine's *Rights of Man*.
◆ **1793–1802** War between Britain and France.
◆ **1800** Act of Union with Ireland unites Parliaments of England and Ireland.
◆ **1803** Beginning of Napoleonic Wars.
◆ **1805** Nelson destroys French and Spanish fleets off Trafalgar, but is killed during the battle.

◆ **1808–14** Peninsular War to drive the French out of Spain.
◆ **1810** Final illness of George III leads to his son becoming Regent in 1811.
◆ **1812** Prime Minister Spencer Perceval is assassinated in the House of Commons by a disgruntled bankrupt.
◆ **1813** Jane Austen's *Pride and Prejudice* is published.
◆ **1815** The defeat of Napoleon Bonaparte at

Waterloo marks the end of the Napoleonic Wars.
◆ **1815** Corn Laws passed by Parliament protect British agriculture from cheap imports.
◆ **1818** The King's wife, Queen Charlotte, dies.
◆ **1818** Publication of Mary Shelley's *Frankenstein*.
◆ **1819** Peterloo Massacre, in Manchester, of political reform campaigners.
◆ **1820** Death of King George III, aged 81 years.

GEORGE IV

1820–1830

ALTHOUGH HIS REIGN was notable for the granting of political rights to Catholics, George IV is best remembered for his years as Prince of Wales. During that time he was a great patron of the arts, but led an immoral life. His marriage to Caroline was troubled, and the couple parted amid accusations of infidelity.

☙ BIOGRAPHY

◆ **Born** St. James's Palace, 12 Aug 1762, eldest son of George III and Queen Charlotte.
◆ **Married** Maria FitzHerbert, Park St., Mayfair, 15 Sept 1785; Caroline of Brunswick, St. James's Palace, 8 April 1795, 1 daughter.
◆ **Acceded** 29 Jan 1820.
◆ **Crowned** Westminster Abbey, 19 July 1821.
◆ **Died** Windsor, 26 June 1830, aged 67.

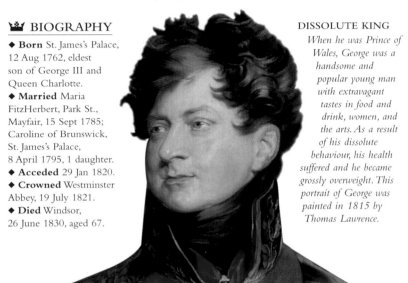

DISSOLUTE KING
When he was Prince of Wales, George was a handsome and popular young man with extravagant tastes in food and drink, women, and the arts. As a result of his dissolute behaviour, his health suffered and he became grossly overweight. This portrait of George was painted in 1815 by Thomas Lawrence.

EVENTS OF THE REIGN

◆ **1820** George IV accedes to the throne, having spent the last nine years as Prince Regent for his blind and deranged father.
◆ **1820** A radical plot to murder the Cabinet, known as the Cato Street Conspiracy, fails.
◆ **1820** Trial of Queen Caroline, in which George IV attempts to divorce her for adultery.
◆ **1821** Queen Caroline is excluded from coronation.

◆ **1823** The Royal Academy of Music is established in London.
◆ **1823** The British Museum is extended and extensively rebuilt to house expanding collection.
◆ **1824** The National Gallery is established.
◆ **1825** Nash reconstructs Buckingham Palace.
◆ **1825** The Stockton and Darlington Railway is opened, the world's first railway service.

◆ **1825** Trade unions are legalized.
◆ **1828** Duke of Wellington becomes British Prime Minister.
◆ **1829** The Metropolitan Police Force is set up by Robert Peel.
◆ **1829** The Catholic Relief Act is passed, permitting Catholics to become Members of Parliament.
◆ **1830** George IV dies at Windsor, aged 67.

WILLIAM IV

1830–1837

A s George III's third son, William IV did not expect to accede to the throne, but he finally became monarch in 1830 at the age of 64. He acquitted himself well as King, showing the good sense to accept advice from his ministers during a period of great political and constitutional reform.

♚ BIOGRAPHY

- **Born** Buckingham Palace, 21 Aug 1765, third son of George III and Queen Charlotte.
- **Married** Adelaide of Saxe-Meiningen, Kew Palace, 13 July 1818.
- **Acceded** 26 June 1830.
- **Crowned** Westminster Abbey, 8 Sept 1831.
- **Died** Windsor Castle, 20 June 1837, aged 71.

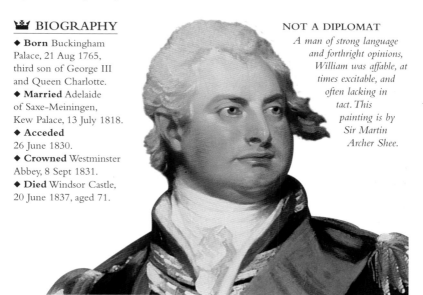

NOT A DIPLOMAT
A man of strong language and forthright opinions, William was affable, at times excitable, and often lacking in tact. This painting is by Sir Martin Archer Shee.

EVENTS OF THE REIGN

- **1830** William IV succeeds his brother, George IV.
- **1831** The new London Bridge is opened over the River Thames.
- **1832** The First Reform Act is passed, extending the vote to a further 500,000 people and redistributing Parliamentary seats on a more equitable basis.
- **1833** Abolition of slavery throughout the British Empire.

- **1833** Factory Act passed, prohibiting children aged less than nine from working in factories, and reducing the working hours of women and older children.
- **1834** Poor Law Act is passed, creating workhouses for the poor.
- **1834** The Tolpuddle Martyrs are transported to Australia for attempting to form a trade union.
- **1834** Fire destroys the Houses of Parliament.

- **1835** The Municipal Reform Act is passed, requiring members of town councils to be elected by ratepayers and councils to publish their financial accounts.
- **1836** Births, marriages, and deaths must be registered by law.
- **1837** Dickens publishes *Oliver Twist*, drawing attention to Britain's poor.
- **1837** William IV dies at Windsor Castle.

VICTORIA

1837–1901

QUEEN VICTORIA SUCCEEDED to the throne at the age of 18, on the death of her uncle, William IV, in 1837. Happy to escape the over-protective environment of her mother, Victoria took on her responsibilities with enthusiasm. Guided initially by Lord Melbourne – the first of many able Prime Ministers – she also received support and advice from her beloved husband, Prince Albert, whom she married in 1840.

PRIVATE GRIEF

In 1861 Prince Albert died of typhoid. His premature death at the age of 42 devastated the Queen, and she went into mourning, refusing to appear in public, seeing all state papers in private, and living in virtual seclusion. The public became disenchanted with such an excessive period of mourning, and there were calls for her abdication.

THE AFFECTION OF THE NATION

Encouraged by her family, friends, and the newly elected Prime Minister, Disraeli, Victoria finally emerged from mourning in 1874. She showed a renewed zest for activity: she attended state balls and made appearances around the country. By the time of her Golden Jubilee in 1887, Victoria had won back the affection of her people, and her 50 years of rule were marked by celebrations throughout the Empire. When she died in 1901, the nation went into deep mourning at the loss of a much-loved monarch.

EVENTS OF THE REIGN 1837–1863

- ◆ **1837** Victoria succeeds her uncle, William IV.
- ◆ **1838** Publication of People's Charter. Start of Chartism.
- ◆ **1840** Victoria marries Prince Albert of Saxe-Coburg-Gotha.
- ◆ **1840** The Penny Post is introduced.
- ◆ **1841–6** Sir Robert Peel becomes Prime Minister.
- ◆ **1845–9** Irish Potato Famine kills more than a million people.

- ◆ **1846** Repeal of the Corn Laws.
- ◆ **1848** Major Chartist demonstration in London.
- ◆ **1851** Great Exhibition takes place in Hyde Park. Its success is largely due to Prince Albert.
- ◆ **1852** Death of the Duke of Wellington.
- ◆ **1853** Vaccination against smallpox made compulsory.
- ◆ **1853** Victoria uses chloroform during the birth of Prince Leopold.

- ◆ **1854–6** Crimean War fought by Britain and France against Russia.
- ◆ **1856** The Victoria Cross is instituted for military bravery.
- ◆ **1857–8** Indian Mutiny against British rule.
- ◆ **1859** Publication of Charles Darwin's *The Origin of the Species*.
- ◆ **1861** Prince Albert dies.
- ◆ **1863** Edward, Prince of Wales, marries Alexandra of Denmark.

IN MOURNING
Victoria was devoted to Prince Albert, and after his death in 1861 she wore black for the rest of her life.

👑 BIOGRAPHY

◆ **Born** Kensington Palace, 24 May 1819, daughter of Edward, Duke of Kent and Victoria of Saxe-Coburg-Saalfield.
◆ **Acceded** 20 June 1837.
◆ **Crowned** Westminster Abbey, 28 June 1838.
◆ **Married** Prince Albert of Saxe-Coburg-Gotha, St. James's Palace, 10 Feb 1840, 9 children.
◆ **Died** Osborne House, Isle of Wight, 22 Jan 1901, aged 81.

EVENTS OF THE REIGN 1863–1901

◆ **1863** The Salvation Army is founded.
◆ **1867** The Second Reform Bill doubles the franchise to two million.
◆ **1867** Canada becomes the first independent dominion in the Empire.
◆ **1868–74** Gladstone becomes Prime Minister for the first time.
◆ **1869** The Irish Church is disestablished.
◆ **1870** Primary education becomes compulsory.

◆ **1871** Trade Unions are legalized.
◆ **1872** Secret voting is introduced for elections.
◆ **1874–80** Disraeli becomes Prime Minister for the second time.
◆ **1875** Suez Canal shares purchased for Britain.
◆ **1876** Victoria becomes Empress of India.
◆ **1884** Third Reform Act further extends franchise.
◆ **1886** First Irish Home Rule Bill fails to pass House

of Commons. Gladstone resigns as Prime Minister.
◆ **1887** Victoria celebrates her Golden Jubilee.
◆ **1887** Independent Labour Party is founded.
◆ **1893** Second Irish Home Rule Bill fails to pass the House of Lords.
◆ **1897** Victoria celebrates her Diamond Jubilee.
◆ **1899–1902** Boer War in South Africa.
◆ **1901** Queen Victoria dies, aged 81.

EDWARD VII

1901–1910

EDWARD VII DID NOT ACCEDE to the throne until the relatively late age of 59. As Prince of Wales, he undertook many duties for his mother, Queen Victoria, making frequent goodwill visits at home and abroad. He was a popular and respected king throughout his reign, and his love of foreign travel and public ceremonial pioneered an ambassadorial style of monarchy that was to replace its earlier political role.

EDWARD AND ALEXANDRA

Edward married Princess Alexandra, elder daughter of King Christian IX of Denmark, in 1863. Alexandra was both elegant and beautiful, and their relationship has been described as "affectionate". Despite this, Edward indulged in many affairs with actresses and society beauties throughout his marriage. However, his wife showed amazing tolerance of his behaviour, remarking that "he always loved me the best".

A LIFE OF LEISURE

Edward VII spent many years as King-in-waiting, only ascending the throne when he was 59 years old. As a result, much of his life was devoted to enjoyment rather than work, and he was renowned as a good-humoured seeker of pleasure. Edward's sporting interests included yachting, shooting, hunting, and horseracing, and he owned many horses, including one Grand National winner and three Derby winners.

EVENTS OF THE REIGN 1901–1908

- ◆ **1901** Edward VII becomes King on the death of his mother, Queen Victoria.
- ◆ **1901** Australia is granted dominion status.
- ◆ **1902** Arthur Balfour becomes Prime Minister.
- ◆ **1902** Edward VII institutes the Order of Merit.
- ◆ **1902** Empire Day is celebrated for the first time.
- ◆ **1902** Rudyard Kipling's *Just So Stories* published.
- ◆ **1903** Wilbur and Orville Wright of the US make the first aircraft flight.
- ◆ **1903** The Women's Social and Political Union, demanding votes for women, is founded by Mrs. Emmeline Pankhurst.
- ◆ **1904** Britain and France sign the Entente Cordiale, settling outstanding territorial disputes.
- ◆ **1904** Sigmund Freud publishes *Psychopathology of Everyday Life*.
- ◆ **1904** *Peter Pan* by J. M. Barrie is published.
- ◆ **1905** Motor buses are first used in London.
- ◆ **1907** Edward VII visits Czar Nicholas II of Russia.
- ◆ **1907** Taxi-cabs are legally recognized in Britain for the first time.
- ◆ **1907** Parliament rejects Channel Tunnel scheme.
- ◆ **1907** New Zealand is granted dominion status.
- ◆ **1908** Production of Ford motor cars begins.

♛ BIOGRAPHY

- **Born** Buckingham Palace, 9 Nov 1841, eldest son of Queen Victoria and Prince Albert.
- **Married** Alexandra of Denmark, 1863, St. George's Chapel, Windsor, 6 children.
- **Acceded** 22 Jan 1901.
- **Crowned** Westminster Abbey, 9 Aug 1902.
- **Died** Buckingham Palace, 6 May 1910, aged 68.

IN LATER YEARS
Being short in stature, and possessing a weak chin, the King's appearance improved greatly with age and the addition of a beard.

EVENTS OF THE REIGN 1908–1910

- **1908** Publication of *The Wind in the Willows* by Kenneth Grahame.
- **1908** The fourth Olympic Games are held in London.
- **1908** Herbert Henry Asquith becomes Liberal Prime Minister.
- **1908** The Triple Entente is signed between Russia, France, and Britain.
- **1908** The Children's Act establishes separate juvenile courts to try children.

- **1908** Contributory Old Age Pension Scheme is established in Britain.
- **1909** The People's Budget is introduced by Lloyd George.
- **1909** The Women's Suffrage movement becomes more militant.
- **1909** Introduction of Labour Exchanges.
- **1909** French airman, Louis Blériot, makes the first cross-Channel flight from Calais to Dover.

- **1909** Selfridges store is opened in London.
- **1909** First rugby football match to be played at Twickenham takes place.
- **1909** First Boy Scout Rally is held at Crystal Palace, London.
- **1910** Constitutional Crisis is caused by the House of Commons' attempt to curb the power of the House of Lords.
- **1910** Edward dies at Buckingham Palace.

CHAPTER TEN

THE HOUSE OF WINDSOR

1910–

G EORGE V CHANGED HIS GERMAN surname of Saxe-Coburg-Gotha to Windsor during World War I, in recognition of the vociferous anti-German feelings of the British people. It was a popular gesture by a conscientious King.

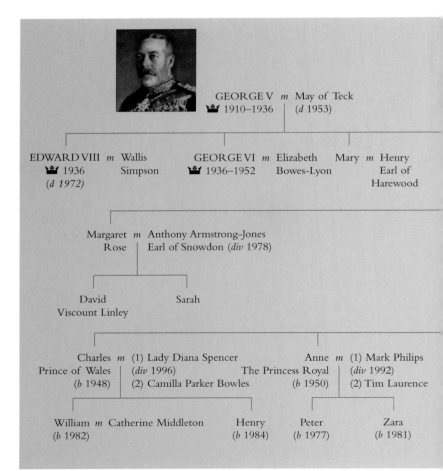

GEORGE V *m* May of Teck
👑 1910–1936 | (*d* 1953)

EDWARD VIII *m* Wallis
👑 1936 | Simpson
(*d* 1972)

GEORGE VI *m* Elizabeth
👑 1936–1952 | Bowes-Lyon

Mary *m* Henry
Earl of
Harewood

Margaret *m* Anthony Armstrong-Jones
Rose | Earl of Snowdon (*div* 1978)

David
Viscount Linley

Sarah

Charles *m* (1) Lady Diana Spencer
Prince of Wales | (*div* 1996)
(*b* 1948) | (2) Camilla Parker Bowles

Anne *m* (1) Mark Philips
The Princess Royal | (*div* 1992)
(*b* 1950) | (2) Tim Laurence

William *m* Catherine Middleton
(*b* 1982)

Henry
(*b* 1984)

Peter
(*b* 1977)

Zara
(*b* 1981)

ROYAL MARRIAGES

The House of Windsor has long been troubled by affairs of the heart. Controversy erupted in 1936 when Edward VIII decided to abdicate rather than give up the woman he loved, Mrs. Wallis Simpson. Although greatly loved and respected, the present Queen, Elizabeth II, has seen recent decades of her long reign troubled by undignified scandals, particularly concerning the doomed marriage of the Prince of Wales and Lady Diana Spencer. Her children have been groomed to uphold the dignity and honour of the monarchy, but their marital difficulties have contributed to a sharp decline in the popularity of the Royal Family. For the first time in a century, the very future of the monarchy itself has been called into question.

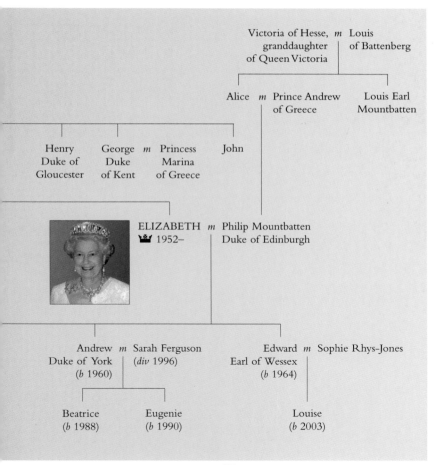

Victoria of Hesse, *m* Louis
granddaughter of Battenberg
of Queen Victoria

Alice *m* Prince Andrew   Louis Earl
of Greece   Mountbatten

Henry   George *m* Princess   John
Duke of   Duke   Marina
Gloucester   of Kent   of Greece

ELIZABETH *m* Philip Mountbatten
1952–   Duke of Edinburgh

Andrew *m* Sarah Ferguson   Edward *m* Sophie Rhys-Jones
Duke of York   (*div* 1996)   Earl of Wessex
(*b* 1960)   (*b* 1964)

Beatrice   Eugenie   Louise
(*b* 1988)   (*b* 1990)   (*b* 2003)

GEORGE V

1910–1936

THE SECOND SON OF EDWARD VII, George became his father's heir when his elder brother, Eddy, unexpectedly died in 1892. He was crowned in 1910, and within four years was King of a country fighting for its survival during World War I. The post-war years were equally turbulent, with war in Ireland, a general strike, world depression, and the formation of a national government, all requiring steady leadership from the King.

WORLD WAR I

Although George and his family had German blood and were related to the German Kaiser, Wilhelm II, George had no compunction at all about fully supporting his government's decision to go to war with Germany in 1914. When Wilhelm abdicated in 1918, George noted in his diary that "he has ruined the country and himself. I look upon him as the greatest criminal known for having plunged the world into this ghastly war".

MAY OF TECK

Princess May was first engaged to Prince Albert Victor ("Eddy"), the elder son of King Edward VII. After Eddy's sudden death in 1892, she married his brother, the future King George V, the following year at St. James's Palace, and she reigned with him as Queen Mary from 1910. The King and Mary enjoyed a long and happy marriage, and had six children. Queen Mary outlived her husband, dying in 1953.

EVENTS OF THE REIGN 1910–1918

- ◆ **1910** George V becomes King and Emperor of India on the death of his father, Edward VII.
- ◆ **1911** Parliament Act ensures the sovereignty of the House of Commons.
- ◆ **1911** National Insurance Act provides sickness and unemployment benefits.
- ◆ **1912** The luxury passenger ship *S.S. Titanic* sinks on her maiden voyage, drowning more than 1,500 people.

- ◆ **1914** Anglican Church in Wales is disestablished.
- ◆ **1914** Outbreak of World War I.
- ◆ **1914** Battles of Mons, the Marne, and Ypres.
- ◆ **1915** Second Battle of Ypres. Allied Gallipoli expedition fails to remove Turkey from the war.
- ◆ **1916** Battle of the Somme. Naval battle off Jutland between British and German fleets results in stalemate.

- ◆ **1916** Easter Rising in Dublin in support of Irish independence.
- ◆ **1916** David Lloyd George replaces Asquith as Prime Minister.
- ◆ **1917** Battle of Passchendaele.
- ◆ **1917** Russian Revolution leads to the abdication of the Tsar.
- ◆ **1918** The end of World War I.
- ◆ **1918** Reform Act gives votes to women over 30.

♛ BIOGRAPHY

◆ **Born** Marlborough House, London,
3 June 1865, second son of Edward VII and Alexandra.
◆ **Married** May of Teck, St. James's Palace,
6 July 1893, 6 children.
◆ **Acceded** 6 May 1910.
◆ **Crowned** Westminster Abbey, 22 June 1911.
◆ **Died** Sandringham,
20 Jan 1936, aged 70.

THE FIRST WINDSOR
George changed his surname from Saxe-Coburg-Gotha to Windsor in response to anti-German feeling during World War I. He enjoyed a successful marriage and a rewarding family life.

EVENTS OF THE REIGN 1918–1936

◆ **1918** General Election produces landslide victory for Sinn Fein MPs in Ireland, who refuse to take their seats in Westminster and form their own Dail parliament in Dublin.
◆ **1919** Lady Astor becomes the first woman MP to take her seat in the House of Commons.
◆ **1920–21** Ireland partitioned into the Free State and the province of Northern Ireland.

◆ **1920** George V unveils the Cenotaph in Whitehall.
◆ **1924** First Labour government formed by Ramsay MacDonald.
◆ **1926** General Strike fails to reverse wage cuts and imposition of longer hours.
◆ **1928** All women over the age of 21 get the vote.
◆ **1928** George V falls seriously ill with blood poisoning of the lung.
◆ **1931** The Statute of Westminster recognizes

independence of the dominions.
◆ **1931** Great Depression leads to the formation of a national government of all three political parties under the leadership of Ramsay MacDonald.
◆ **1932** George V makes the first annual Christmas broadcast on radio.
◆ **1935** George V celebrates his Silver Jubilee.
◆ **1936** George V dies at Sandringham.

EDWARD VIII

January–December 1936

WHEN EDWARD SUCCEEDED George in January 1936, he determined to marry Mrs. Wallis Simpson, a twice-divorced American. This provoked a constitutional crisis. Baldwin informed Edward that the country would not accept her as Queen. After deliberation, he abdicated in December 1936.

♛ BIOGRAPHY

◆ **Born** Richmond, Surrey, 23 June 1894, eldest son of George V and May of Teck.
◆ **Acceded** 20 Jan 1936.
◆ **Abdicated** 11 Dec 1936.
◆ **Married** Wallis Simpson, Maine-et-Loire, France, 3 June 1937.
◆ **Died** Paris, France, 28 May 1972, aged 77.

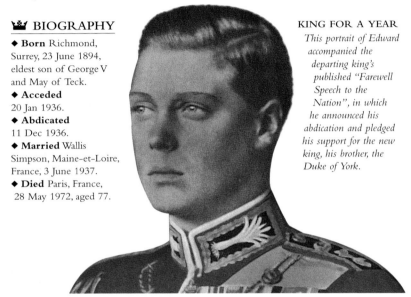

KING FOR A YEAR
This portrait of Edward accompanied the departing king's published "Farewell Speech to the Nation", in which he announced his abdication and pledged his support for the new king, his brother, the Duke of York.

EVENTS OF THE REIGN

◆ Edward VIII succeeds his father, George V, as King on 20 January.
◆ Outbreak of the Spanish Civil War.
◆ Germany, under Adolf Hitler, reoccupies the demilitarized left bank of the Rhine.
◆ Britain begins to rearm as political tension increases in Europe and the prospect of military conflict in the region becomes more evident.

◆ Fire destroys Crystal Palace, once the home of the Great Exhibition in Hyde Park but now located in Sydenham, south London.
◆ J.M. Keynes publishes his book *General Theory of Employment, Interest and Money*, an internationally influential study of modern economics.
◆ Maiden voyage of luxury ocean liner, the *Queen Mary*, takes place.

◆ The BBC inaugurates the world's first television service at Alexandra Palace in London.
◆ On 10 December Edward signs the Instrument of Abdication. Witnessed by all his brothers, it is a simple declaration of his intent to renounce the throne for himself and all his descendants. He is subsequently created Duke of Windsor.

GEORGE VI

1936–1952

EDWARD VIII'S UNPRECEDENTED abdication resulted in George VI becoming King without any preparation for the role. Yet he became a popular figurehead for the nation during World War II, led Britain into the post-war era, and restored the reputation of the monarchy after Edward's abdication.

♛ BIOGRAPHY

- **Born** London, 14 Dec 1895, second son of George V and May of Teck.
- **Married** Lady Elizabeth Bowes-Lyon, Westminster Abbey, 26 April 1923, 2 daughters.
- **Acceded** 11 Dec 1936.
- **Crowned** Westminster Abbey, 12 May 1937.
- **Died** Sandringham House, Norfolk, 6 Feb 1952, aged 56.

WAR-TIME KING

George VI was a good athlete and a brave soldier – he fought in the Battle of Jutland – but there was a diffident and anxious side to his character, which exhibited itself in an acute stammer. However, once the kingship was thrust upon him, he showed his determination and inner resolve by mastering his speech impediment.

EVENTS OF THE REIGN

- **1936** George VI accedes to the throne upon the abdication of his brother, Edward VIII.
- **1938** Prime Minister Neville Chamberlain signs agreement with Hitler at Munich in attempt to stop outbreak of war in Europe.
- **1939** Outbreak of World War II.
- **1940** Retreating British troops evacuated from beaches of Dunkirk as Germans advance.
- **1940** Winston Churchill becomes Prime Minister.
- **1940** Battle of Britain fought in the skies over England between RAF and German Luftwaffe.
- **1941** US enters War after Japanese air raid on US fleet at Pearl Harbor.
- **1942** Decisive British victory at El Alamein.
- **1944** D-Day landings in Normandy as the Allies begin to push the German forces back across Europe.
- **1945** The defeat of Germany marks the end of the War in Europe.
- **1945** Japan surrenders, after US drops atomic bombs on its cities.
- **1947** India and Pakistan granted independence.
- **1948** National Health Service establishes free medical treatment.
- **1951** Winston Churchill becomes British Prime Minister again.
- **1952** George VI dies.

ELIZABETH II

1952–

THE REIGN OF ELIZABETH II is one of the longest in British history. She began her reign as Britain was emerging from a period of post-war austerity and had begun to relinquish its empire. Britain's role in the world has now changed irrevocably, while the country itself has undergone a radical transformation. In recognition of this, the Queen has attempted to modernize the monarchy without weakening its authority.

FORMAL ROLE

As the head of one of the few constitutional monarchies in the world, the Queen's role is largely formal. Regal ceremonies have remained mostly unchanged over the centuries, as have her responsibilities to Parliament, the armed forces, Church, and state. Yet as head of state she also has to respond to events and changes whenever they occur around the world, dealing with matters of diplomacy as well as national state events.

FAMILY LIFE

The Queen's devotion to duty has brought much support and public affection to her and her family, evident in the excitement created by the marriage of her grandson, Prince William, in April 2011 and in anticipation of a Diamond Jubilee celebrating her 60 years on the throne. However, the turbulent lives of the Queen's children, and the expense of running the royal family, has led to criticism about the role of the monarchy itself.

EVENTS OF THE REIGN 1952–1972

- **1952** Elizabeth accedes to the throne on the death of her father, George VI.
- **1953** Edmund Hillary and Tenzing Norgay climb Mount Everest just before Coronation Day.
- **1955** Winston Churchill resigns as Prime Minister and is succeeded by Anthony Eden.
- **1956** Anglo-French forces invade Egypt after the nationalization of the Suez Canal.
- **1957** Harold Macmillan becomes Prime Minister.
- **1957** The Gold Coast becomes independent as Ghana, the first British colony in Black Africa to receive its independence.
- **1959** Oil is discovered in the North Sea.
- **1960** Harold Macmillan makes "winds of change" speech in South Africa.
- **1963** Alec Douglas-Home replaces Harold Macmillan as the
- Prime Minister.
- **1963** The Beatles release their first LP.
- **1964** Labour government of Harold Wilson takes office.
- **1969** Charles is invested as Prince of Wales.
- **1969** Troubles break out in the north of Ireland.
- **1970** Conservatives return to power under Edward Heath.
- **1971** Decimal currency is introduced.

LONG TO REIGN

Observers say that even as a child, Elizabeth was grave, reserved, and wise beyond her years. The long duration of her reign has made Elizabeth utterly professional, ever mindful of the seriousness of her role, and rather shy. However, as shown from countless private photographs, she is not averse to spirited laughter.

♛ BIOGRAPHY

◆ **Born** Bruton Street, London, 21 April 1926, eldest daughter of George VI and Lady Elizabeth Bowes-Lyon.
◆ **Married** Philip Mountbatten, Westminster Abbey, 20 Nov 1947, 4 children.
◆ **Acceded** 6 Feb 1952.
◆ **Crowned** Westminster Abbey, 2 June 1953.

EVENTS OF THE REIGN 1973–

◆ **1973** Britain joins the European Community.
◆ **1974** Harold Wilson returns as Prime Minister.
◆ **1979** Margaret Thatcher succeeds James Callaghan, becoming Britain's first woman Prime Minister.
◆ **1981** Prince Charles marries Lady Diana Spencer at St. Paul's Cathedral.
◆ **1982** Britain goes to war with Argentina over control of the Falkland Islands (Las Malvinas).
◆ **1990** Margaret Thatcher resigns as Prime Minister after 11 years.
◆ **1991** The Allied forces liberate Kuwait during the Gulf War.
◆ **1996** Both the Prince and Princess of Wales, and the Duke and Duchess of York divorce.
◆ **1997** The Labour Party ends 18 years of Conservative government.
◆ **1997** The Princess of Wales dies in Paris car crash.
◆ **2002** Princess Margaret dies in February; the Queen Mother in March, aged 101.
◆ **2010** Conservatives and Liberal Democrats form first coalition government since 1940.
◆ **2011** Prince William marries Kate Middleton in Westminster Abbey; Britain prepares to celebrate the Queen's Diamond Jubilee on the throne, and host the Olympic Games in 2012.

THE FUTURE KINGS

RINCE CHARLES IS well aware of his responsibility to ensure that his son and heir, Prince William, is groomed for his future role as king. Charles takes that responsibility seriously, and brought his own experiences as Prince of Wales to bear on the upbringing of both Prince William and his younger brother, Prince Harry.

CHARLES AND DIANA
Prince Charles and Lady Diana married at St. Paul's Cathedral in 1981. The couple had two sons, William and Harry, but their marriage formally ended in 1996.

WILLIAM AND KATE
Prince William became engaged to Kate Middleton in October 2010, when he presented her with his mother Diana's sapphire and diamond engagement ring.

INDEX

ACKNOWLEDGMENTS

The publisher would like to thank the following for their kind permission to reproduce their photographs:

c = centre
b = bottom
l = left;
r = right
t = top

akg-images: 91 c. Ancient Art & Architecture Collection: 24 c. Barnaby's Picture Library: 11 cr;

12 tr. Bridgeman Art Library, London/New York: 25 c, 30 c, 33 clb, 34 c, 41 c, 49 cr. British Library: 28 tl. E.T. Archive: 14 cl, 16 c. Corbis/The Print Collector: 89 cl. Corbis/ Tim Graham: 87 cl, 93 tc. Eton College Library: 37 tc. Getty Images: 94b, Tim Graham 94 cl. Mary Evans Picture Library: 90 c. Robert Harding Picture Library: 70 c. Robert Harding Syndication /IPC Magazines Ltd: Blairs College, Aberdeen 63 cr. Michael

Holford: 13 cr, 27 c, 31 c. Hulton Getty: 83 tl. Illustrated London News Picture Library: 86 cl. National Library Of Scotland: 56 cl. National Portrait Gallery: 29 c, 33 br, 35 c, 38 br, 38 c, 40 c, 44 cl, 44 bl, 46 c, 49 cl, 51 c, 53 tc, 64 bl, 64 cl, 67 tl, 69 cr, 71 c, 72 cl, 72 c, 73 c, 76 c, 77 c, 79 tc, 80 c, 81 c, 85 tc; Scala: 54 -55, 62 cl. Scottish Record Office: Duke of Buccleuch 57 tr. Walker Art Gallery: 47 c, 48 tl. Zefa Picture Library: 59 cr.